Creating your own
SOFT FURNISHINGS

Creating your own

SOFT FURNISHINGS

Angela Fishburn

A practical guide to ideas and techniques

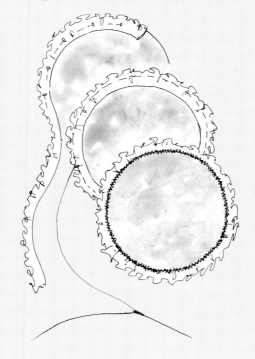

Holt, Rinehart and Winston · New York

First published in the United States in 1986 by
Holt, Rinehart and Winston, 383 Madison Avenue,
New York, New York 10017.

Library of Congress Cataloging in Publication Data

Fishburn, Angela.
Creating your own soft furnishings.

Includes index.
1. House furnishings. 2. Sewing. Interior decoration – Amateurs' manuals. I. Title.
TT715.F59 1986 656.2'1 85-11210
ISBN: 0–03–008513–6

First American Edition

Printed in Italy
1 3 5 7 9 10 8 6 4 2

ISBN 0-03-008513-6

Contents

Introduction
With a Guide to Basic Techniques 7

Sewing Guide
With Hints on Care and Repair 107

Acknowledgements 111

Index 112

Introduction
With a Guide to Basic Techniques

Soft furnishings play a more important role in our lives than most of us realize, colour and texture influencing us deeply, often without our being aware of it. A bright, lively decorative scheme will be exciting and stimulating, while a quiet, restful one aids relaxation. This versatility provides the opportunity to create whatever background we feel suits our way of life.

Homes, like people, should be dressed with style and imagination. The beauty of designing and making your own soft furnishings is that it offers the chance to create something original and individual. Good features can be emphasized and enhanced, others less attractive can be cunningly disguised.

Before you start it is wise to sit back and consider carefully the following points. If you are to be successful there is a lot of planning to do before you go out and buy anything – lists to make, samples to collect and budgets to draw up. Don't make the mistake of rushing into a major purchase without giving yourself plenty of time to consider the alternatives. It will be time well spent and you will be amply rewarded by the finished result.

First decide on the style you like and establish your ideal objective. This of course will be governed by what the room is to be used for as well as personal preferences on other factors such as colour, shape and texture. When you are sure in your own mind of what you like and feel comfortable with, you can make a decision and stick to it. Once you have identified an objective everything else should fall logically into place.

Begin by making a sketch of each room to scale, marking in any existing furniture. Make a folder to hold paint charts and all the samples of wallpaper, flooring and fabrics that you consider suitable for major items such as covers and curtains. Start a scrapbook of ideas inspired by effective room-sets seen in the glossy magazines, store window displays and on television to help you decide on the effect you are trying to create.

Do not worry if you cannot achieve everything at once. It is much better to start with the basics and get them right, then add to them gradually. You may have to make a temporary compromise with some features but if you always keep your main objective in mind you should not stray too far from your original idea.

If you are working to a tight budget it is often possible to start with cushions or other small accessories once you have a good idea of what you are aiming at. It is surprising what a difference a new tablecloth or lampshade makes.

Furnishing on a budget is certainly a challenge but it is one you will find worthwhile and enjoyable once you explore the possibilities of making your own soft furnishings. Whether you simply smarten up a room with a few new tablecloths and cushions or tackle major items such as covers and curtains, it brings a wonderful sense of achievement too.

COLOUR, SHAPE AND TEXTURE

The colour wheel (fig 1) is the starting point to help you choose colours and put them together successfully. Study it and you will see that it is divided into two – one half providing the warm colours (reds and yellows), and the other the cool colours (greens and blues). Start by choosing a colour that you and your family like and work round it; bear in mind the aspect of the room, remembering that warm colours work well in north- and east-facing rooms while cooler colours are more suited to south- and west-facing rooms. You will find that tones of colours change with the movement of the sun during daylight hours, and are similarly affected by how much artificial light is used. 'Tone' is the amount of light reflected back from a colour, and is greatly influenced by the background to that particular colour as well as any objects surrounding it. That is why it is so important to look at fabrics,

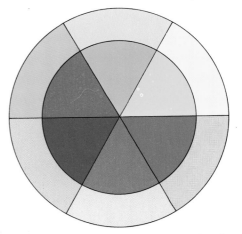

fig 1 The colour wheel can be an invaluable aid when planning the decor of your room

Opposite: Plump cushions, frilled blinds and layers of tablecloths give a relaxed air to a room where patterns and plains are boldly mixed in positive colours

wallpapers, flooring, lampshades and so on in both daylight and artificial light in the position you are thinking of using them.

Experiment by placing small samples of fabric on to backgrounds of various colours. Observe how different the samples look depending on the surrounding colour. Sometimes the colour of the fabric will appear lighter, sometimes darker. It is very important to notice these differences if you are to achieve the effect you want.

Light colours can be used to create an effect of spaciousness or to highlight certain areas, while dark colours tend to make rooms look smaller and are useful for disguising features such as a too-high ceiling or an uneven wall.

The amount of one particular colour used is also of importance and can create illusions of shape and size. Too much of a single colour (or pattern) on one side of the room can upset the balance of your scheme. So careful thought should be given to the position and amount of each colour used.

When choosing a colour from the colour wheel, look either side of it to find which colours will work well with it and harmonize. When these colours are used together this is called a 'related' scheme and usually has a restful effect. Those that are opposite to it on the wheel are 'complementary' and can also be used successfully for contrast. It is the shades that are neither opposite nor next to your chosen colour that will be 'discordant' and which will jar the eye.

You can use one colour on its own effectively; this is called a 'monochromatic' scheme. In this case it is necessary to use several different tones and textures of the one colour to provide interest and variation. A contrasting or 'accent' colour is often used for one or two small accessories to give the scheme impact.

Texture and shape are as important as colour when planning a room scheme. Upholstery, carpets, floors and furniture should provide a good balance of texture and colour. Choose your soft furnishings to complement them.

A room decorated exclusively with shiny surfaces or knobbly tweeds would look very dull and uninteresting; it is better to aim for a contrast of textures, especially if you are using a limited palette of colours.

Highly polished furniture can be softened by choosing a soft velvet or patterned cotton print for your upholstery rather than shiny leather or plain chintz. Floors can be hard varnished wood, soft shiny vinyl or carpeted in all kinds of plains and patterns from smooth velvet through short and looped tufts to the luxury of long-pile shag.

Add interest to your walls by using a textured wallpaper: rough hessian, suede or leather effect, shiny satin, real wool strands or grasses in a matching or complementary colour. Windows can be softly draped with curtains, lace and festoons or crisp and practical with wooden shutters or roller blinds, while cushions and rugs are an excellent way of adding a change of texture without a major investment of cash. Make your cushions soft and squashy in velvet, cotton and satin, or smart, well-stuffed box and sausage shapes for a tailored look; rugs in wool, tweed or ethnic weaves add a personal touch to walls, floors and even sofas.

Look out for shapes too. If your decorative scheme is beginning to look like a series of straight lines and box shapes, introduce a few curves – a circular rug or table, a well-curved lampshade or round cushions, perhaps a more softly shaped sofa. Introduce a plain surface or change of pattern among your wallpapers and fabrics. Do not forget to change the scale too: a complementary small print will offer relief in a scheme using mainly bold patterns, while a large design in small doses on a feature wall, as a border, on cushions, curtains or chairs adds impact to an understated decor.

Before you make a final decision on the design of your room it is also worth experimenting with new positions for chairs, tables and other movable pieces of furniture, using paper cut-outs on your scaled room plan. It is surprising how different the shapes of familiar furniture can look in a new arrangement.

United by a warmly toned pattern, the awkward corners of a small room live in harmony, offset by plain white paint and polished pine

CHOOSING FABRICS FOR SOFT FURNISHINGS

There is such a wide range of fabrics now available, such a rich selection of colours, patterns and textures, that it is often very difficult to know where to start. The best way is to visit shops that specialize in soft furnishing fabrics, for there you will find experienced assistants to guide you if necessary, and answer questions on the composition, pattern printing, quality and practicality of the fabrics you would like to use.

Consider carefully the following points when selecting fabrics:

● Choose the best quality fabrics you can afford, and the ones that offer the best value for money. Some of the less expensive fabrics are quite suitable for children's rooms, where they may easily get torn or stained and need to be replaced more often. In bedrooms, where they will not be subject to heavy wear and tear, less durable fabrics will suffice; but do not cut back on quality for such things as loose covers on armchairs. This is false economy, as they will soon need replacing.
● When choosing fabric for soft furnishings, make sure that it suits the purpose for which it is needed. This means selecting practical, hardwearing fabrics for kitchens, living rooms and halls. Check that they are easily washable or that they can be dry cleaned. Textured fabrics attract dirt and dust more easily than smooth-surfaced ones, which means that they will need more washing or cleaning. Curtains and blinds in kitchens often get dirty fairly quickly, so make sure that the fabrics used here are easily washable or at least spongeable.
● Dress fabrics can sometimes be used for items such as lampshades and scatter cushions, but they are not usually suitable for curtains and covers. They are not made to withstand the long exposure to light and atmosphere that soft furnishings get, nor are they as durable and hardwearing. Since dress fabrics are made in narrower widths, more seams would be needed to make large items.

● Check fabrics to see whether they are fade- and shrink-resistant. The type of dyeing process used determines how resistant a fabric is to light. When fabrics are subjected to strong sunlight it is wise to use a protective lining. Alternatively, incorporate a blind or sheer curtain when choosing a style for windows. If you are making unlined curtains remember that they will have no protection from strong sunlight and other atmospheric conditions.
● Ask for samples of fabrics so that you can look at them carefully at home in the appropriate setting in both daylight and artificial light. Sometimes it is even worth buying a metre of the fabric to make quite sure that it is suitable. This can then be

A perfect blend of traditional and modern, the comfy sofa covered in an easy-to-live-with print, windows artfully draped with polka-dot voile

tested for washing, creasing and pressing. You can also make sure any pattern is printed accurately and whether it is likely to pull out of shape as you work with it. This piece need not be wasted. It can often be used later for making smaller accessories – perhaps a cushion or a lampshade.
● Fabrics for curtains should drape well to be effective. Ask to see the material draped so that you can check the impact of both the colour and the pattern. Make sure that the pattern you have chosen does not disappear in the fabric's folds.

● When choosing loose-cover fabric make sure that it is closely woven, hard-wearing and washable. Preferably choose small print designs, random match patterns or textured fabric; these are easier to handle when making up. Try to avoid large patterns, which are often wasteful because of pattern matching.

● When buying fabric check for flaws, which should be marked on the selvedge with strands of coloured cottons. When you get the fabric home unroll it to check that it is perfect, without snags, pulls, or shade variation. Do not cut the fabric until you have done so, as shops cannot be expected to make allowances for imperfections on cut fabric.

● Buy fabric from one roll only, and enough to finish the project. Colour dyes vary with each batch. It may not be possible to obtain the exact match later. If necessary, place a special order so that all the fabric comes from the same roll.

● Make sure when choosing a patterned fabric that the pattern is printed accurately on the straight grain of the fabric. Unless the pattern has been woven into the fabric it is likely to be slightly off grain in most cases, and at an angle to the warp and weft threads. This presents particular problems when making up curtains as the fabric will not hang or drape properly unless it has been cut to the grain. To test this, fold back a small piece of the fabric from selvedge to selvedge with wrong sides together, and check whether the

fig 2 Checking that the pattern runs along the straight grain

pattern runs correctly along the fold (fig 2). Often the degree of inaccuracy is almost unnoticeable and would not be important, but where it is, a different fabric should be chosen in order to avoid disappointment with the finished result. If in doubt, check with an experienced sales assistant before a purchase is made.

● Light colours, loose weaves, and sheer fabrics allow more light to filter through than heavily textured, closely woven fabrics.

● Any lined curtain will provide more insulation than an unlined one.

● Interlined curtains and thermal linings are useful in children's bedrooms if noise and light are a problem, for they are particularly effective at blocking out sound and glare. They are essential for curtains with an exceptionally long drop for them to hang correctly. Remember, though, that an interlined curtain must be dry cleaned and cannot be washed.

● Small floral random repeat patterns and geometrics work well in small rooms.

Use fabric lavishly to give a soft and feminine effect, choosing small prints in restful colours and introducing curved lines wherever possible

Keep patterns in proportion to the size of rooms, restricting the use of very large ones to spacious rooms.

● Stripes, spots and geometrics co-ordinate well with many different fabrics, whether patterned or plain.

● Take particular care when mixing fabrics that they relate and balance well in both colour and design.

● Keep abreast of current trends in furnishing fabrics by constantly looking out for good design, whether in shops, in magazines, brochures or books. These are all wonderful sources of inspiration; train your eye to analyse and assess good design and you will be well on the way to developing a sense of style of your own.

● A word about cost. When working to a limited budget never economize on the amount of fabric needed. Choose a less expensive one instead.

FABRICS AND THEIR MAKE-UP

Furnishing fabrics are usually made up from two basic components – man-made fibres and natural fibres. Man-made fabrics are manufactured by using raw materials such as minerals and vegetables and chemically treating them to produce a fabric which often looks and feels very similar indeed to its 'natural fibre' counterpart. It does not follow, however, that the care of these fabrics is the same, so individual washing and dry cleaning instructions should be followed carefully. Fabrics often react in very different ways to heat and temperature conditions.

Natural fibres, such as silk, wool, cotton and linen are frequently blended with man-made fibres to create hardwearing, practical fabrics, ideal for soft furnishings. 'Stable' fibres will keep their dimensions after laundering, dry-cleaning, and during wear. 'Durable' fabrics will keep their colour and surface quality over time.

Fabric fibres and their characteristics
Acetate (synthetic) This is a stable and durable fibre which has good insulating qualities. Care is needed with washing as it becomes weaker when wet and also when exposed to strong sunlight. It resists dirt and dust well and melts rather than burns if subjected to high temperatures.

Acrylic (synthetic) This is a stable and durable fibre that resists strong sunlight. It is non-absorbent and will not shrink or stretch when washed. It will melt rather than burn at high temperatures.

Cotton (natural) These fibres are stable and durable and can be printed and dyed easily. Cotton can be treated with many different finishes to make it shrink- and fade-resistant, as well as crease-resistant and water-repellent. It will burn at high temperatures unless specially treated.

Linen (natural) Strong and durable, linen resists dirt well and does not shrink. Because it creases easily it is often blended with other fibres such as cotton or polyester to improve its appearance and make a hardwearing furnishing fabric.

Nylon (synthetic) This is stable and hard-wearing but will fade in strong sunlight. It will not crease and resists dirt and dust well. It will melt rather than burn if exposed to high temperatures.

Polyester (synthetic) This is strong and durable, washes well and is shrinkproof. It will withstand strong sunlight, resists dirt and dust well and is crease-resistant.

Rayon viscose (synthetic) This is a non-stable fibre, often blended with others to make it sunfast and crease-resistant.

Silk (natural) This is a natural fibre which is expensive to produce. It is stable and durable and dyes well. It washes well and has an attractive natural sheen that many other fabrics lack. Silk fibres are strong but will fade and rot if exposed to strong sunlight.

Wool (natural) This is strong and durable and very resilient. It dyes well and can be treated to make it shrink-resistant. It also blends well with synthetic fibres to make a crease-resisting fabric.

THE WORKBOX

Here is a list of essential tools and equipment for making your own soft furnishings. Most of them are usually readily available in any household. Remember to replenish the workbox regularly with new pins and needles, as these can rust and will easily mark new fabrics. Keep all scissors well sharpened and make sure that you have a good quality pair of cutting-out shears, an expensive item but one which is well worth the money invested.

Needles Include different-sized needles for a variety of fabrics and threads.
  Sharps and Betweens: Useful for general work.
  Crewel/Embroidery: A longer eye makes these easier to thread with thicker threads and embroidery cottons.
  Mattress needles: Curved needles useful for repairs.
  Bodkins: Useful for threading elastic, cords and tapes through casings.

Pins Good quality steel dressmaking pins will last longer and give good service. Glass-headed pins can be used for lampshades but extra care is needed when using them as they are very sharp.

Threads Match the thread to the fabric colour, choosing a slightly darker shade. When working with patterned fabric use a thread that matches the dominant colour. Use synthetic threads with man-made fibres, and cotton or multi-purpose cotton-coated polyester threads with natural fibres. Use size 40 for heavy fabrics, size 50 for medium and lightweight fabrics, and silk or No 60 cotton for finer fabrics. Invest in a large reel of tacking cotton for basting; it will be economical in the long run.

Scissors Choose good quality scissors and keep them well sharpened. Ideally, have a pair of cutting-out shears 20·5-23cm (8-9in) long and a small pair about 13-14cm (5-5½in) long for general use.

Thimble Metal thimbles give the best protection. Thimbles are essential as it is often necessary to push the needle through several layers of fabric. It is quicker and easier to sew firm lampshades and coarse materials if a thimble is used. Try to get used to wearing one.

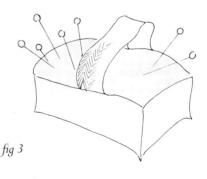

fig 3

Weight Cover a brick or an old iron with fabric, making a handle with upholstery webbing (fig 3). Use this when making curtains and blinds to prevent the fabric slipping from the work surface. If the top of the brick is padded it can double as an extra pin cushion.

Cutting-out surface. Use a large table for cutting out. A wallpapering table makes a useful cutting-out surface when preparing and making curtains and other large items. Do not be tempted to use the floor; apart from making fabric dirty, it is uncomfortable to work on and can be damaging both to the back and the knees.

Sewing machine A sewing machine is necessary for dealing with the many long seams used in soft furnishings. It should have a presser foot attachment that enables it to stitch close to the piping cord when making cushions, loose covers, and so on. A simple zigzag facility is also useful and makes it easy to neaten seams and edges. An electric or treadle machine leaves both hands free to control the work.

Iron and ironing board See notes on pressing and ironing on page 110.

Measure As well as a fibreglass or linen tape measure, invest in a wooden metre or yard stick. Inexpensive ones are generally available from good wallpaper shops and they are an invaluable aid to measuring and making curtains when a rigid rule is essential. A large set square is also very useful when cutting out lengths of fabric.

Tailor's chalk Use white (which is the easiest to remove) and one other colour. Never use ordinary pencil or biro on furnishing fabrics.

Upholstery pins and skewers These are useful for holding fabric in position when making loose covers.

Notebook This is invaluable for jotting down measurements, making cutting plans and working out requirements of fabric. Keep it in a safe place with the rooms clearly marked and you will not have to do all your calculations again when you refurnish.

CURTAINS

Curtains play an important part in any decorative scheme but they also have two other important functions – to provide privacy and insulation.

Making curtains yourself is a great money saver as lined and interlined curtains are particularly costly to have made

fig 4

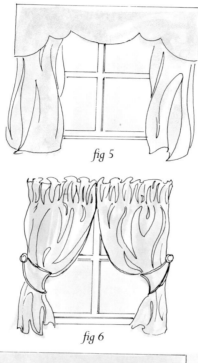

fig 5

fig 6

fig 7

professionally. Gain confidence by tackling the smaller projects first and then progress to the ones that present more problems. Remember that all you really need is a little time and patience, and a knowledge of the sewing skills necessary to create a professional finish.

If possible find a good flat surface on which to work. Wallpapering and table-tennis tables, or even a large piece of plywood or chipboard placed on a covered dining room table, give plenty of space. It is worth taking the time to organize your work space before you start.

Choose a style
Windows lend themselves to many different treatments. When deciding which you like best, look at the various effects that can be achieved by the use of the many tracks, fittings and heading tapes now available. Optical illusions can be created and faults hidden by making the window look wider, shorter, smaller or larger (figs 4-7).

An inescapable feature of many modern homes is the presence of a radiator under the window which can be a difficult obstacle to overcome when choosing curtains. Shorter curtains overlapping the radiator by about 5cm (2in) are best to prevent wasteful heat loss but if you really want a more formal look why not make floor-length dress curtains held to the side with tie-backs (page 71) and have a matching festoon blind for screening the window after dark.

The style of curtains is crucial to the mood of a room and usually provides a large expanse of its colour and texture. Floor-length curtains look elegant in living rooms and dining rooms, while short, frilled curtains look pretty and cosy, especially in, say, a bedroom.

Tracks and fittings
Buy tracks and fittings from a shop that specializes in them such as a good hardware shop or department store where they are well displayed, and all the information you need about their practicality and use made readily available. Many helpful booklets are produced by the

manufacturers of particular tracks and accessories. Have a good look at them before you make your final choice.

Some tracks are not very sturdy and are not meant to take the weight of heavy curtains; others have cording systems so that the curtain fabric is not handled too much in use. Some tracks have combined hooks and runners, and some are easier to fix than others. All these points need checking carefully to avoid disappointment later.

Linings

Linings extend the life of curtain fabrics by protecting them from sun, frost and other temperature changes as well as minimizing damage caused by dirt and dust. They also help the curtains to drape well, giving them body and fullness, and give a pleasantly uniform appearance to the outside of a house.

Most curtain linings are made from cotton sateen. This is a closely woven fabric available in a wide range of colours as well as in white and natural. Choose the best quality lining you can afford as it will be less likely to shrink when washed or dry cleaned. As lining sateen is not evenly woven, do not try to tear it when cutting out. Cut it cleanly with shears. An aluminium-coated lining fabric is also available which has good insulating properties, useful when light and noise are a problem.

Detachable linings can be used for sheer open-weave fabrics. They are easily removed for washing and can be changed from one pair of curtains to another. They do not drape as well as permanently lined curtains but are a useful alternative in some situations: where curtains have to be frequently washed for example, or where curtains are changed for a heavier weight material in the winter months.

Interlining a curtain gives it a luxurious look as well as providing good insulation and draping qualities. It keeps the cold out and the warmth in and gives the fabric extra body. Interlining is also useful for reducing noise from outside as well as cutting out more light. This makes it particularly useful for bedrooms. Use bump or domette for interlining. This

soft, loosely woven fabric is an ideal choice, but a flannelette sheet can be used as an economical alternative.

Although interlining adds to the cost of curtains, its insulating properties make it well worth the extra expense and work involved – and it is far less expensive than double glazing.

Heading tapes

The style of heading chosen will depend on the effect you wish to achieve, and on your budget. Some of the commercially gathered and pleated heading tapes require more fabric than others. Simple standard gathering tape is less expensive than the more elaborate ones and requires much less of the main fabric. You will have to choose the style of heading before estimating the amount of fabric you need to buy, for this determines the fullness of the curtain and, consequently, the number of widths of fabric needed for each curtain. Consider also the effect of fullness on the fabric pattern.

Simple curtain gathering tape This requires one and a half times the width of the track and is perfectly adequate for use on curtains which will be positioned underneath pelmets or window valances.

Pencil pleats These are produced by pulling up cords on specially constructed tape and the fabric needs to be two and a half times the width of the track to be effective.

Pinch pleats The pleating on some tapes is achieved by inserting single, double or triple pleater hooks into the tape at regular intervals, thus reducing the curtain width to the size required. An alternative type of commercial tape uses draw cords to produce sets of pleats automatically. These tapes require the fabric to be two and a half to three times the width of the track.

Alternatively, a hand-made heading can be substituted using buckram or other stiffened fabric. (See instructions for making buckram-headed curtains on page 103). Use the guide above when estimating fabrics for these headings.

Measuring and estimating for curtain fabrics

When you have chosen the style and headings for your curtains and the tracks and accessories have been fitted, you can estimate the fabric requirements and select a suitable material.

1 Measure the width of the track or pole, and decide where the curtains will hang and what their finished length will be (fig 8). These two measurements determine the amount of fabric needed. Use your notebook to record the measurements.

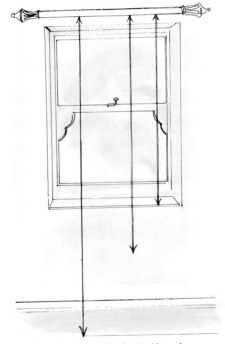

fig 8 Measuring for the finished length

2 Decide on the fullness needed for the curtain heading and calculate from this the number of widths that will be required. It is often necessary to join widths and half widths together to obtain the required measurement. Half widths should be placed at the outer sides of the window. Remember that light, unlined fabrics generally require more fullness than heavy interlined ones, and that thick lined curtains need more room at the sides when they are drawn back.

3 Take the measurement from the track to the finished length of the curtain. Add to this a 15-23cm (6-9in) allowance on each drop for hems and headings.

4 If a patterned fabric is chosen allow an extra pattern repeat per drop of curtain to enable the pattern to be matched satisfactorily. Pattern repeats should start at the lower edge of the curtain after an allowance of 64-75mm (2½-3in) has been made for the hem (fig 9).

5 Allow the same amount of lining and interlining fabric as for the curtains unless the fabric varies greatly in width.

6 With the measurements obtained in (2) and (3) above make a plan on paper. This will show you at a glance how many metres of fabric are required. If patterned fabric is being used remember to add to the calculations one pattern repeat for every drop of curtain cut after the first one. For example a curtain needing three widths of fabric will require an extra allowance of two pattern repeats. Always err on the generous side, and work to the nearest half width or 0·5m (½yd) depth.

Cutting out lengths of curtain fabric
When you are sure you have the correct amount of fabric and have assembled all the necessary tape headings, thread and materials, you are ready to make a start on cutting out.

1 Unroll the fabric and lay it on a large working surface, checking it for flaws and imperfections. A large square or rectangular table or worktop enables the fabric to be squared up easily.

2 To make the first cut, start at the lower edge of the curtain length. Make a seam allowance of 64-75mm (2½-3in) for the hem and, if possible, draw a thread to obtain a straight line across the grain on which to cut. The line should be at right angles to the selvedge. Draw a line across the fabric width using a rigid rule and tailor's chalk. Cut along this line. Plain fabrics should always be cut to the grain, but where a printed fabric is slightly off-grain follow the line of the pattern instead. A pattern that is badly off-grain should not be used (see notes on pages 9 and 10 on choice of fabrics).

fig 9 Allowing for pattern repeat

fig 10 Cutting the first length

fig 11 Matching pattern repeats

3 Measure and mark the length of the first width of fabric with pins and a rigid rule. Draw a line across the pin line with tailor's chalk and cut (fig 10).

4 Cut out the next and subsequent lengths of fabric, taking care to match the pattern repeats and allow for turnings (50-75mm (2-3in) at the lower edge, 12·5-15cm (5-6in) at the top edge) (fig 11). Mark the top of each length with tailor's chalk as it is cut, to make sure that all lengths hang in the same direction. This is particularly important when working with velvets and other fine-textured fabrics.

5 Cut off all selvedges, for these often make the curtain seams pucker. If the fabric frays badly, snip the selvedges instead at 50mm (2in) intervals to prevent it from pulling.

Fitting heading tape
Heading tapes control the gathering and hang of the finished curtain and are available in a wide range of styles. Costs vary according to type but avoid the very cheapest unbranded standard tapes as the draw cords tend to snap when gathered.

1 Measure the width of the curtain to see how much tape is required, and allow 50mm (2in) at each end for turnings.

2 Size up the curtains by measuring them with a rigid rule from the bottom hem to the top edge where the tape will be positioned. Some heading tapes have rows of pockets so that the headings can be adjusted if necessary after the curtains have been finished, but try to be as accurate as possible when taking measurements and positioning the tape. The tape is sewn into position approximately 6mm (¼in) from the top edge of the curtain. Fold excess lining and fabric into the top edge of the curtain. This allows the curtain to be lengthened from the top at a later date if necessary without there being an ugly mark at the hem.

3 Pin and tack the tape into position along the top edge of the curtain, turning in

13mm (½in) at each end. Machine the tape, working the stitching along the top edge first, then the lower edge. Work both in the same direction to prevent the tape from puckering. Complete the stitching at the side edges.

4 Pull out the draw cords at each end of the tape, tying and knotting one end securely. Insert the hooks and draw up the tape, distributing the gathers evenly along the top of the curtain. Do not trim off any of the cords but tie them neatly at the end of the curtain or use a special cord tidy. They can then be released when the curtains need to be cleaned.

LOOSE COVERS

Loose covers can be made for many different styles of chairs and sofas, as well as for divans, day beds and ottomans. They are not usually suitable for buttoned upholstery, however.

Making a loose cover for a chair or sofa protects it from dirt and dust. It is also a useful way of updating and renovating a worn chair. If properly made, a loose cover gives an upholstered appearance to a chair but, unlike a fitted cover, is easily removed for washing or cleaning.

Before making a loose cover check first that the upholstery and structure of the chair is sound. A cover is only as good as its foundation, and it will not disguise or remedy sagging springs and worn webbing. Remove as much dirt and dust as possible from the existing covering or it will quickly work through the new fabric and damage its fibres.

A loose cover should be made by cutting pieces of fabric and pinning the sections together so that they fit the shape of the chair. This is a more successful method than using a paper pattern or cutting out fabric from an old cover.

Choose fabrics for loose covers that are firm, smooth and closely woven as these will give the maximum amount of wear. They should be crease- and shrink-resistant, hardwearing and washable. Linen union, twill and tightly woven cot-

tons as well as some man-made fabrics make successful covers. Loosely woven fabrics are not suitable, as they quickly lose their shape. Also avoid thick heavy fabrics. These are difficult to handle when several layers have to be fed through the machine, and are more suited to tightly fitted upholstered covers.

Choose small print designs or random match patterns; since these present few problems with pattern matching they are therefore more economical to make up. Larger patterns need to be centred in many places on a loose cover and therefore require more fabric.

Buy the best quality fabric you can afford, and be generous when measuring and estimating for fabric. Any that is left over can easily be used for making extra cushions or arm caps, which will extend the life of a loose cover quite considerably. Spare fabric can also be used for repairing and renovating the cover when it wears to make it last a little longer.

Piping This is used to define the outline of the chair and also to provide strength to the seams. The fabric used for covering the piping cord should be similar in weight and texture to the chair cover but can be in a contrasting or co-ordinating

fabric. Boil the piping cord and dry it thoroughly before use. This prevents it from shrinking when the cover is washed and so puckering the seams. About 10-12 metres (11-13yds) of No. 3 piping cord is needed for an average-sized chair cover.

Tuck-away This is the extra fabric that is allowed on each section of the cover where it is tucked into the seat. It helps the cover to stay firmly in place.

Arm caps Arm caps are made in the same way as the loose cover, piping the seams and making 13mm (½in) double hems at the edges. These useful extras long extend the life of a loose cover.

Openings The opening for the loose cover is always positioned at one of the back seams and should be finished with a facing before hooks and bars or touch-and-close fastener are applied to close it (see instructions for *Boxed cushions*, page 54). Alternatively, use a zip, but make sure that it is a very strong one for the opening takes considerable strain when the cover is put on and taken off.

In a grand room a number of large patterns can be employed with confidence, with borders of different kinds for emphasis

MEASURING FOR LOOSE COVERS

As a rough guide, the amount of 120cm (48in) wide fabric needed for a loose cover is five times the height of the back of the chair. When using patterned fabric allow an extra metre of fabric. An average-sized chair will require approximately 7 metres (7¾yds) of fabric, but to obtain a more accurate estimate take the following measurements and add them together.

1 From the bottom of the outside back over the top of the chair and down into the inside back, plus 50mm (2in) for turnings and 15cm (6in) for tuck-away.

2 From the back of the seat to the bottom of the front section, plus 50mm (2in) for turnings and 15cm (6in) for tuck-away.

3 From the bottom of the outside arm, over the arm and into the inside arm to the seat, plus 50mm (2in) for turnings and 15cm (6in) for tuck-away. Double this measurement to allow for two arms.

Add to this estimate 1 metre (1¼yds) for making bias strip to cover the piping cord, 2-3 metres (2½-3½yds) for the frill (depending on the style chosen) and an extra 1 metre (1¼yds) of fabric for each loose cushion cover. Allow 0.5 metre (½yd) for each arm cap. Two sets of seat cushions and arm caps adds considerably to the life of a loose cover.

TRADITIONAL LAMPSHADES

Effective and attractive lighting is an important but often neglected feature of home design. Choose lamps and fittings to suit both function and setting; successful lighting can add another dimension to your scheme, creating different moods by flattering and emphasizing specific areas and objects.

Fabrics
Soft lampshades are made using translucent fabrics such as silks and satins. Other suitable fabrics include lightweight fur-

nishing cottons and dress fabrics. Thick, heavy fabrics will not do as not enough light filters through for them to be effective. Do not use fabrics that are flammable nor any that would melt if placed too near to a naked bulb.

Use light colours for shades intended for reading or study, and darker ones for a more relaxing or moody, dramatic effect.

Fabrics with plenty of 'give' or elasticity are most successful as they are easier to handle. Less flexible fabrics tend to get wrinkled. Choose crêpe de Chine, silks, shantung, fine cottons, crêpe-backed satin, ginghams, polyester/cotton sheeting, broderie Anglaise, lace or lawn. Do not use fabrics that split or fray easily.

Most soft lampshades look best lined. The lining covers the struts, reflecting the light as well as diffusing it softly.

Estimate the amount of fabric needed by measuring the depth of the frame plus 10cm (4in) and the circumference of the largest part of the frame (usually the bottom ring) plus 12.5cm (5in). Cut the fabric in two pieces if necessary.

A lampshade in matching fabric adds a masterly finishing touch to a scheme, especially where the basic colour is an unusual lilac

Frames
Choose a frame made from a firm strong wire, one that is both free from rust and rough edges. If possible, select frames that have a plastic coating, as these do not rust and need little preparation. Favourite old frames can be re-covered successfully with fresh fabric provided they are not bent or out of shape. This fault is one which is very difficult to remedy. If using an old frame, remove all the binding tape and check that the frame is not rusty. If it is not coated with a plastic finish, rub it with fine glasspaper and paint it with a quick-drying enamel or gloss paint. Leave until the paint is quite hard before attempting to re-cover the frame.

Lampshade frames are made with different fittings and come in many sizes and shapes. They are measured across the base ring at their widest point. Check that the fitting is suitable for your lamp.

Binding tape

Use 13mm (½in) cotton lampshade tape or soft unbleached loosely woven tape. This can be easily dyed to the colour of the lining with a cold-water dye – which is useful when making lampshades where the struts will show, for example, in a Tiffany style. To estimate the amount needed, allow twice the circumference of the top and bottom rings and twice the length of each strut to be bound. Do not bind gimbal or pendant fittings with tape.

Binding the frame well is important because the fabric will be pinned and stitched to the tape. Make sure that it is taut and smooth on struts and rings alike to prevent it from showing through the fabric on the finished lampshade..

When using plastic-coated frames, bind the top and bottom rings and any struts where pinning and sewing will take place. On other frames all struts must be bound, to protect them from rusting.

Trimmings

A trimming conceals visible stitches and sometimes covers seams. Its choice is governed by the style of the lampshade and the texture of the fabric. Use silky braids and fringes on silk and other delicate fabrics and keep plainer, more coarsely woven ones for furnishing and dress cottons. Alternatively, make a bias strip in matching or contrasting fabric, or make a simple frill to trim the lower ring.

Braids and fringes should be stitched to the lampshade wherever possible, but frills and bias strips should be applied with a clear quick-drying adhesive.

FIRM LAMPSHADES

Quick and easy to make, firm lampshades are well suited to modern rooms.

Buy specially prepared lampshade card or prepare it yourself using your own fabric or wallpaper. You can do this by bonding it to a special PVC material which has an adhesive on one side. Tear off the protective backing and press your material smoothly on to the sticky surface.

White buckram can also be used as a backing for fabrics. Dampen it and iron the fabric on to it with a hot iron. Cover the fabric with a damp cloth and iron again. Let it dry thoroughly before use.

Keep trimmings plain and simple, such as velvet ribbon and those made on the cross from matching or contrasting fabric (see *Cutting fabric on the bias grain* – Sewing Guide, page 109), applied with a good clear-drying adhesive.

Do not wash firm lampshades but keep them clean by regular brushing.

Choosing a base

The lampshade should balance well with the base and be well proportioned. As a guide, the diameter of the lampshade should be approximately the height of the base; or the height of the lampshade should be slightly less than the height of the base (fig 12). The base must be heavy enough to support the shade without fear of tipping over (this could be a fire hazard!).

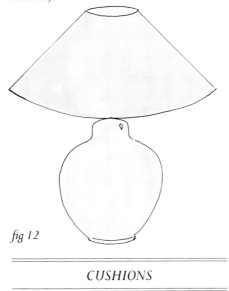

fig 12

CUSHIONS

Small cushions are pretty home accessories which look stylish in both living rooms and bathrooms. They are costly to buy but can easily be made at home, often from remnants of fabrics left over from other projects. Choose co-ordinating fabrics in similar textures and weights. Frills can vary in width but generally a 64-75mm (2½-3in) frill looks effective, with piping in a contrasting colour to add interest.

Choose a cushion pad with one of the following fillings, or make one yourself if you already have a suitable filling available:

Feather and down This is an ideal filling for scatter cushions as well as for loose cushions for the seats of sofas and chairs. It is soft and resilient and wears well. Use featherproof ticking or downproof cambric if making a cushion pad, to prevent the filling from working through the cover fabric. Make sure that the fabric chosen for the pad will not show through the cushion cover. Make the pad 13mm (½in) larger all round than the outer cushion cover so that the cushion has a well filled appearance.

Synthetic wadding This is produced from man-made fibres such as Courtelle, Dacron and Terylene, and is light in weight. The filling is washable. Some are allergy free, which makes them ideal for anyone allergic to feathers or down. To make a fully washable pad, choose an easy care fabric such as polyester/cotton.

Kapok This is a lightweight, inexpensive filling suitable for cushions both indoors and out. It is non-absorbent but not as longlasting as some other fillings, as it tends to go lumpy with wear. Use calico or sheeting when making a cushion pad.

Large floor cushions are best covered in strong fabrics and carry bold patterns and strong colours well. Cover the inner pad with strong cotton fabric or calico. Synthetic wadding is the best filling. Otherwise use either of:

Plastic foam chips Foam chips do not have the smooth appearance of the latex and plastic foams. This inexpensive filling can also be used for garden cushions because the chips do not absorb moisture. Make the inner cushion casing from a strong calico or cotton fabric.

Latex and plastic foam This is made in various shapes and sizes and in different qualities. It is easily obtainable and can be cut to the exact size required with a very sharp knife. Cover it with calico or cotton before putting on the outer case to protect it from crumbling with wear.

Fresh, Young and Bright

LINED CURTAINS WITH HEADING TAPE
PIPED LOOSE COVER FOR AN ARMCHAIR
ROUND FRILLED CUSHION
PLAIN SQUARE CUSHION
CONICAL LAMPSHADE

*Primary colours need not look over-bright and brash
if you blend them skilfully. Here, red, white and blue have been cleverly
used with shocking pink to create a young but sophisticated living room
where a hot, predominantly red, pink and white fabric adds warmth and
colour to a soft blue and white scheme. The tailored blue loose cover on
the armchair with its contrasting pink piping offers exactly the right
balance between defined shape and softness — a feeling echoed in the
clean, simple lines of the two low tables with their subtly rounded edges.
It is this clever combination of curves and strong geometric shape that
helps today's modern furniture and furnishings look smart yet feel
comfortable. Note how the straight lines of chair, tables and storage units
in this room have been balanced by the round shapes of bowls and vases,
the co-ordinating plates on the wall and a pair of contrasting cushions —
plain and square for the patterned, round and frilled for the plain fabric.*

*Simple lined curtains are fresh and unfussy
allowing the strong random pattern of primary splashes to speak for
itself; bold designs such as these will add life and energy to your décor but
they should be handled with care. Use them sparingly and make sure they
are not competing with too many other strong elements of the room. This
scheme works because the cool background of plain blues and clean
whites, with the occasional touch of pink, is the perfect foil for the bright
and breezy pattern of the curtains.*

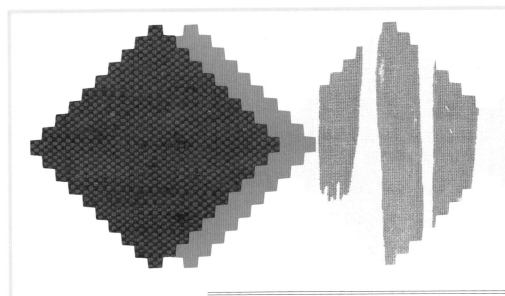

SAMPLES OF THE MATERIALS USED

---

1 Loose armchair cover
Tough, blue upholstery fabric, a washable 51% linen, 49% cotton mix.

2 Round cushion and piping
Washable lightweight polyester cotton poplin in fuchsia pink to provide accent colour and highlight the shape of the chair.

3 Square cushion and curtains
Washable 100% cotton fabric with bold splashes of red, yellow, blue, pink and green.

4 Lampshade
Plain white linen.

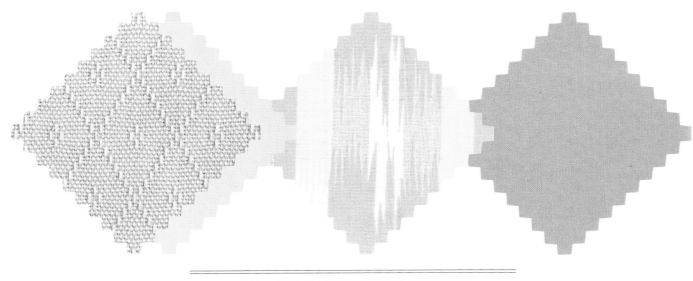

AN ALTERNATIVE COLOUR SCHEME

There is no need to turn to strong colours to devise an adventurous scheme with an up-to-the-minute feeling. A cool palette of ice cream shades in plain and random striped cottons and linens can provide the inspiration for a combination that is just as refreshing but softer and prettier. Duck-egg-blue upholstery fabric with a tiny diamond design, practical, hard-wearing and attractive, adds textured appeal to the armchair, brought into focus with butter yellow chintz piping, repeated on a frilled cushion. The gently patterned cotton print cleverly combines all the colours in the scheme, harmonizing them while introducing a note of excitement. Ideal for sill-length curtains and a matching square cushion, it provides an expanse of imaginatively mixed colour. Pale peach cotton for the lampshade brings a glow by night and day, while the different textures of the plain fabrics add further contrast and interest. Understated as the colours are, the final effect is delectable.

LINED CURTAINS WITH HEADING TAPE

Most curtains need a lining unless they are simply to filter light and are being made from either sheer or semi-sheer fabrics. A lining helps them to drape well and protects them from dirt and dust. Linings give a luxurious feel to all curtains, and their protective qualities can add years to the life of fabrics, a consideration worth remembering when you are working with costly materials.

Apart from the seams and the headings, lined curtains should be made by hand and have a 'locked-in' lining which gives the most satisfactory results. This means the lining is firmly fixed to the curtain fabric so that it does not fall away from it when the curtain is hanging. This also gives the curtains more body.

YOU WILL NEED

Curtain fabric
Matching thread
Lining sateen
Heading tape

To make

1 Estimate the amount of fabric needed following the instructions on pages 15 to 16, and cut it out.

2 Join widths or half widths together where necessary using a plain flat seam. Press open. There is no need to neaten the edges. Where a patterned fabric is used, pin the fabric together carefully matching the pattern repeat and tacking on the outside as shown in fig 11 (page 14).

3 At the side and lower edges of the curtain turn in 38mm (1½in); mitre and stitch the two corners at the lower hem (see Sewing Guide, pages 108-9). Tack the two side hems and the lower hem and serge stitch as in figs 13 and 14.

4 Cut the lining sateen to the exact size of the curtain fabric after cutting off all selvedges. Do not try to draw a thread on

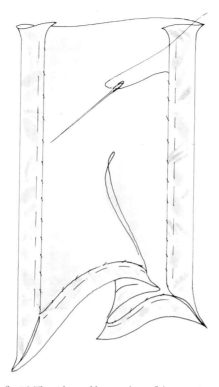

fig 13 The sides and lower edges of the curtain are turned in and the corners are mitred and stitched

fig 14 Sergestitching the raw edges on the hems of the curtain

lining sateen, but instead square it up and cut it against a table. Alternatively, use a large set-square. As lining sateen is not evenly woven, do not try to tear it. Join lining widths, where necessary, with a plain flat seam and press open.

5 Place the curtain fabric on the work surface with the right side down. Lay the wrong side of the lining on to the wrong side of the fabric, matching the sides and lower edges. Fold the lining back and lockstitch into position as in fig 15, working two rows of lockstitch to every width of fabric. Work this from the top to the bottom of the curtain length.

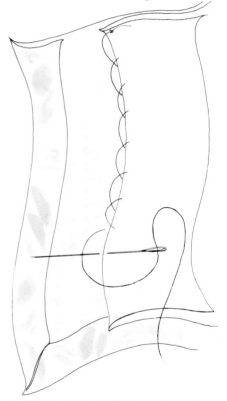

fig 15 Lockstitching the lining to the curtain

6 Fold in the lining 25mm (1in) at the sides and bottom of the curtain. Tack and slipstitch into position.

7 Make a line of tacking stitches across the curtain 15-20·5cm (6-8in) from the top edge to hold the lining in position whilst the heading tape is applied.

8 Follow the instructions for applying heading tape on pages 14-15, press and hang.

PIPED LOOSE COVER FOR AN ARMCHAIR

New loose covers will give a fresh lease of life to your upholstered furniture and are easily removed for cleaning to maintain that freshness. Before you start, check that your chairs are suitable for re-covering by reading the general information on making loose covers on page 15.

YOU WILL NEED

Approximately 7m (7¾yds) fabric 120cm (48in) wide
Matching thread
10-12m (11-13yds) piping cord No 3 (boiled for 5 minutes and dried before use to ensure it will not shrink when cleaned)
10-12m (11-13yds) bias strip
Paper for labelling fabric sections
Tailor's chalk
Upholstery pins or skewers
Zipper foot attachment for machine

Cutting the fabric

1 Measure and estimate the amount of fabric needed as described on page 16.

2 Make small paper labels to pin to each section of the loose cover as you cut it out (fig 16).

3 Measure the chair and divide it in half, marking the line with pins or tailor's chalk (fig 16).

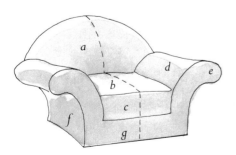

fig 16 a inside back, b seat, c cushion gusset, d inside arm, e front arm, f outside arm, g frill. Some chairs will have a back gusset

4 Remembering to centre any pattern on the fabric, fold the fabric in half with the wrong sides facing, and place this to the centre line on the inside back of the chair. Pin the fabric in position using upholstery pins or skewers (fig 17).

5 Cut out the fabric allowing 50mm (2in) for turnings at the top of the chair and 15cm (6in) for tuck-away at the seat. As you cut each section, mark it with a line or arrow on the wrong side with tailor's chalk to show the lengthwise grain of the fabric to prevent you pulling it off grain when the cover is being constructed.

6 Cut out the fabric for the outside back, seat and front sections in the same way, allowing seam and tuck-away allowances where appropriate. Make sure that the straight of the grain of the fabric runs to the floor otherwise the cover will not fit properly.

fig 17 Pinning the folded pieces to the chair

7 Cut the inside and outside arm sections and the front arm sections from separate pieces of fabric, remembering to add the 50mm (2in) turning allowances and making sure that any pattern repeats are carefully positioned to match correctly.

8 Unpin all sections and make sure a label is attached to each one to identify it.

Fitting the cover

1 Following the lines of the original upholstery of the chair, pin the sections together with the right sides inside. If necessary, trim off some of the excess fabric to fit round the shape of the chair as in fig 18. Make darts if you need to take in any fullness and clip curves to help them lay flat. First pin the bottom of the inside back to the seat allowing 15cm (6in) on each section for tuck-away. Then pin the back, arm and seat sections together.

fig 18 Trimming any excess fabric

2 Pin the cover well, adjusting the pins for a perfect fit. Trim seams to 25mm (1in).

3 Check that the pins are firmly fixed, then remove the cover from the chair. Tack and machine stitch all tuck-away seams and darts.

4 Make approximately 10-12m (11-13yds) of bias strip 38mm (1½in) wide (see page 109, Sewing Guide).

5 Insert the piping and bias strip in the appropriate seams, removing a few pins at a time. Re-pin and tack into position using matching thread so that the stitches do not need to be removed when the cover is completed.

6 If the chair cover needs an opening to enable the cover to be removed easily, position it out of sight in one of the back seams. The opening should measure approximately two thirds of the length of the seam. Mark the position of the opening along the seam and remove the pins. Apply the piping to the outside back as far as the top of the opening then cross over the piping and apply it to the outside arm section so that the opening on the finished cover is well concealed.

7 Tack any remaining seams.

8 Fit the cover on the chair checking the fit and making any necessary adjustments.

9 Mark the position for the frill and pin and tack the bias strip and piping cord on to this line (fig 19).

fig 19 Marking the position for the frill

Machining the cover

1 Machine stitch the piped seams in the following order using a zipper foot attachment: outside arms, front section, front arm, outside back up to the opening.

2 Where two piped seams meet, pull out the cord and cut off 25mm (1in) so that the piping does not overlap and look bulky. Work another row of machine stitching 3mm (⅛in) from the first to give the seams extra strength.

3 Trim seams to 13mm (½in) and neaten with a zigzag stitch.

FRILLS

Most chairs and sofas look more attractive if finished with a frill added to the base of the cover. The frill can be gathered or pleated and should be made up before it is applied to the cover. Instructions for making and applying frills or a simple tie-under finish are given on pages 36-7.

ROUND FRILLED CUSHION

Round or square frilled cushions are surprisingly easy to make using fabric remnants from other projects and can be co-ordinated or contrasted with your main decorative scheme. Choose a light-weight or delicate furnishing fabric when making this type of cushion. Heavy-textured fabrics are not suitable as the frill will not gather well.

YOU WILL NEED

Round cushion pad (see page 29 for instructions on making cushion pads)
Furnishing fabric
Matching thread
Contrasting fabric for bias strip
Piping cord No 2 or 3
(boiled for 5 minutes and dried before use to ensure that it will not shrink when cleaned)
Paper for pattern
Large round tray or plate
Zipper foot attachment for machine

To make

1 Make a circular pattern to the size of the cushion pad using a large round tray or plate to draw a circle. The finished cushion should look plump and comfortable, so take care when measuring the cushion pad that it is cut 13mm (½in) larger all round than the cushion cover to ensure a well-filled appearance.

2 Cut out two pieces of fabric the size of the pattern plus 13mm (½in) allowance for turnings, making sure any design is

centrally placed. Notch grain lines in four places on both sections of the cover (fig 20). If the fabric frays easily, neaten the edges with a zigzag stitch before making up the cushion cover.

3 Prepare enough bias strips 38mm (1½in) wide for piping round the circumference of the cushion. Make this using the method described on page 109.

4 Pin and tack the bias strip and the piping cord to the front section of the cushion cover, clipping this every 38-50mm (1½-2in) to enable the piping to sit well along the curved shape (fig 20).

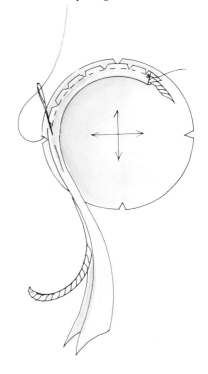

fig 20 Tacking the bias strip and piping cord to the front section of the cushion

5 Cut out and make a double frill in matching or co-ordinating fabric. To make a frill 64mm (2½in) wide (finished measurement) cut a strip of fabric on the straight grain 15cm (6in) wide by one and a half to twice the circumference of the cushion pad. Join the short edges of the strip together with a 13mm (½in) flat seam and press open. Fold the fabric in half lengthwise and work two rows of gathering stitches 6-13mm (¼-½in) away from the raw edges (fig 21).

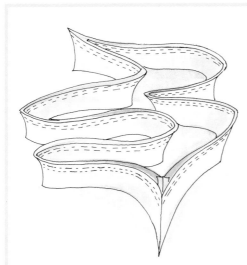

fig 21 For a double-sided frill the loop of fabric is folded in half and gathering stitches are worked along the raw edge

6 Pin and tack the frill to the front section of the cushion cover over the piping cord and bias strip, arranging the gathers evenly round the outer edge of the cushion section (fig 22). Machine into position.

7 With right sides facing, pin and tack the back section to the front section, matching notches on grain lines. Leave an opening of approximately 23cm (9in) at the back of the cushion cover. Machine carefully into position using a zipper foot attachment to enable the stitching to be as close as possible to the piping cord.

8 Neaten the raw edges and turn the cover to the right side. Insert the cushion pad and slipstitch the opening firmly together.

fig 22 Tacking the frill to the front section

SQUARE FRILLED CUSHION

These are made in the same way, using a square pad, but take care when applying the frilled edge to the cushion to allow more fullness at each corner of the cushion so that the frill sits well (fig 23). The opening should be positioned along one side of the cushion cover.

fig 23 Allowing extra fullness at the corner

PLAIN SQUARE CUSHION

Cushion covers made of bold fabrics work best as simple untrimmed squares. Follow the instructions for a *Round frilled cushion* on page 23, but make a square pattern and omit steps 3-6.

CONICAL LAMPSHADE

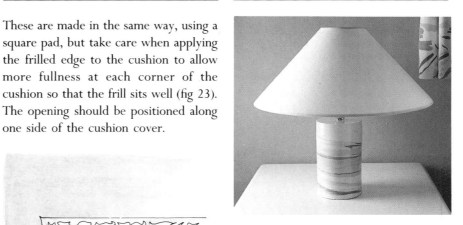

Making your own conical lampshades is an excellent way of using up remnants of fabric for matching or co-ordinating accessories. Inexpensive to make, they are well worth the time spent hand stitching the fabric to the frame.

YOU WILL NEED

Strutted conical lampshade frame
Lampshade tape
Fabric for cover
Matching thread
Stiff paper for making pattern
Clip-on pegs
Good clear-drying adhesive
Trimming or bias strip

To make

1 Choose a strutted frame with either a pendant or a gimbal fitting.

2 Tape the frame as in fig 24 so that you have a firm base on which to sew the cover material. Estimate the amount of tape needed by allowing twice the circumference of the top and bottom rings and twice the length of each strut. Tape each strut first, keeping the tape tight and smooth. Start at the top ring and when the bottom ring is reached, wind the tape first to one side of the strut and then to the other. Finish with a knot around the bottom ring. Trim off the tape. When all the struts have been bound, tape the top and bottom rings in the same way, making a figure-of-eight turn round each join in the struts and ring.

3 Take a piece of stiff paper and make a paper pattern from which to cut out the cover fabric. The amount needed can be estimated only when the pattern has been cut. Make this in two halves allowing 25mm (1in) seam allowances on each half (figs 25 and 26). Fit the pattern to the frame with clip-on pegs and adjust if necessary.

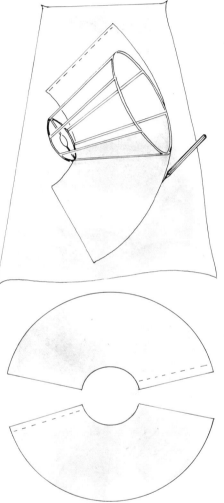

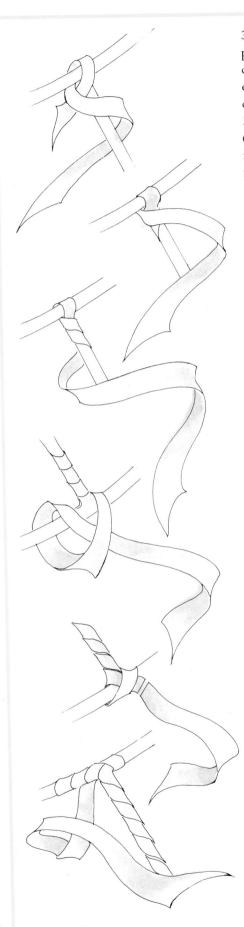

fig 24 Taping the frame

fig 25 and fig 26 Making the paper pattern for a conical lampshade. The pattern is made in two pieces for a snug fit

4 Cut out the cover fabric using the paper pattern and secure firmly to the frame with clip-on pegs (fig 27).

5 Stitch one half of the fabric to the top and bottom rings of the frame, using blanket stitch. Sew through both the fabric and the tape and use a strong short needle with short lengths of double thread.

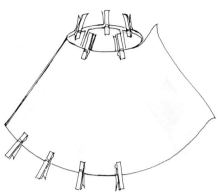

fig 27 Securing the fabric with pegs

6 Stitch the other half of the fabric to the frame in the same way to within 38mm (1½in) of where the seam is to be positioned. Trim off excess fabric, overlap the seam to make it 6mm (¼in) and secure with a clear-drying adhesive. Complete the stitching at the top and bottom rings (fig 28).

fig 28 Stitching the fabric to the frame

7 Fix a trimming to the top and bottom, starting at a side seam. Use a small knife to apply the adhesive. Turn in each end of the trimming 13mm (½in) and butt them together (fig 29). A bias strip in matching or contrasting fabric makes an attractive finish. (See Sewing Guide, page 109.)

fig 29 Applying trimming to the shade

An Invitation to Relax

FLOOR CUSHION WITH PIPED SEAMS
INTERLINED CURTAINS
BOLSTER CUSHIONS WITH PIPED SEAMS
DIVAN COVER
PLAIN SQUARE CUSHION

There is no reason why you should not enjoy the rich
warmth and comfort of a Middle Eastern interior in your own living
room. Here a mixture of fabrics in strong co-ordinating designs of rust
reds and blues is offset by the coolness of plain cream painted walls and
lush green plants.

To achieve that luxurious feeling of richness you
have to be bold in your choice of designs, selecting large patterns and
intricate shapes, and extravagant in your use of fabric – skimping would
only spoil the effect. Curtains should be generous with plenty of width to
drop from ceiling to floor, and interlined to give them weight and body,
as well as help them to hang correctly. A simple divan for relaxing and
reclining can be fitted with a loose cover in a matching or co-ordinating
fabric and smothered in cushions of all shapes and sizes.

Cushions are essential to capture that bedouin atmosphere
and are quick and easy to make at home. Include a couple of floor
cushions – these not only co-ordinate in shape and colour but also,
appropriately enough, feature desert palms in the design – firm bolster
cushions with smart piped seams for supporting your back or head, and
plenty of soft cushions for self-indulgent comfort. When making up the
cushions remember that a strong busy pattern does not generally need
frills and fancy trimmings.

To round off the effect add a suitably ethnic print or poster, a few exotic
plants and a touch of brass for real authenticity.

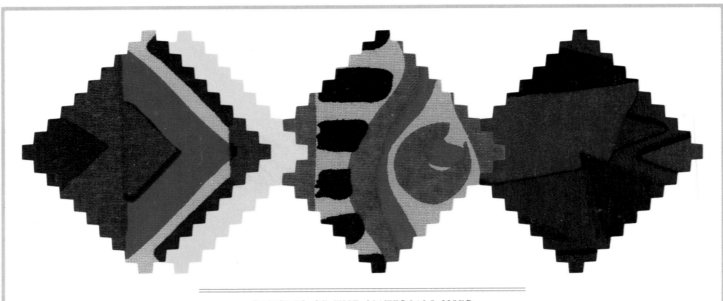

SAMPLES OF THE MATERIALS USED

Three fabrics from one co-ordinated range in 100% cotton. Making covers for the cushions with zip fasteners for easy removal takes advantage of the fact that these fabrics can be washed by hand at low temperatures.

1 Curtains
Venetian red and midnight blue predominate in a print of rich, deep shades accented with deep orange and sand.

2 Wall covering
Cream matt emulsion provides a plain background for the opulent prints.

3 Floor cushions
The brighter hues are used with dash to define an exotic design.

4 Divan cover, bolster and scatter cushions
Deep blue, burnt Siena, plum, in a simple abstract pattern.

AN ALTERNATIVE COLOUR SCHEME

A relaxing atmosphere with a more modern air can be established by using fabrics closely co-ordinated in pattern as well as colour. Deep blue and white always succeeds, smartly adapting itself as well to a small geometric print as to more traditional designs. Including a plain blue in the scheme extends the possible permutations further. In a family room the blue-on-white fabric would make sense for curtains, with brilliant white, spongeable emulsion paint on the walls. Where practicality is less of a consideration, the same fabric would make stunning floor cushions on a shaggy white carpet with curtains in white-on-blue hung in generous folds. Such a colour scheme can be restful but it needs contrast. Use shocking lipstick pink for a dramatic touch: on piping for the plain navy divan and bolster cushions, lavish quantities of scatter cushions and perhaps a pair of shapely ceramic table lamps with sculptured shades to match.

FLOOR CUSHIONS

Seating at floor level creates a casual re-laxed atmosphere well-suited to modern entertaining, and provides an opportunity to use strongly patterned fabrics.

FLOOR CUSHION WITH PIPED SEAMS

YOU WILL NEED

For a floor cushion 90cm (36in) square
2m (2 ¼yds) fabric 120cm (48in) wide
Matching thread
2m (2 ¼yds) calico or strong cotton for covering the pad
4m (4 ½yds) piping cord No 3
(boiled for 5 minutes and dried before use to ensure it will not shrink when cleaned)
Pad or filling
Zipper foot attachment for machine

To make the casing

1 Cut out two pieces of strong calico or cotton fabric 94cm (37in) square.

2 Place the right sides together and tack and machine round the four sides, leaving an opening along one side of approx-imately 30·5-35·5cm (12-14in) to enable the filling to be inserted. Clip across the corners (fig 30) and turn to the right side.

3 Fill the casing with synthetic wadding or foam chips and sew up the opening using oversewing stitches for strength.

fig 30 Clipping the corners of the inner casing before turning to the right side

To make the cushion cover

1 Measure the cushion pad (fig 31) and cut two pieces of the cover fabric the size of the pad. Do not allow any extra for turnings; the cushion will then fit tightly and have a plump appearance.

2 Prepare enough bias strip for piping round the four sides of the cushion using the method described on page 109. Join the bias strip as in figs 32.

3 Pin and tack the bias strip and piping cord to the right side of the front section of the cushion cover, beginning in the centre of one side (fig 33). Machine into position using a zipper foot attachment on the machine.

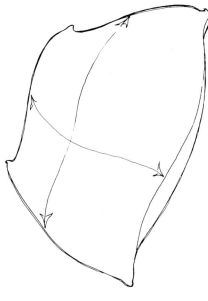

fig 31 Measuring the completed cushion pad

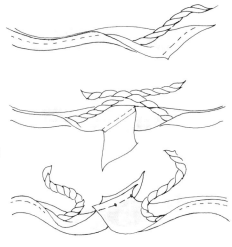

fig 32 Joining the bias strips

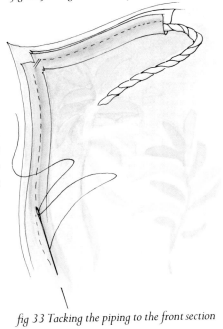

fig 33 Tacking the piping to the front section

4 With right sides together, pin and tack the back section to the front section leav-ing the opening untacked along one side. Machine. Clip the corners as in fig 30 and neaten the seams with a zigzag machine stitch or overcast by hand (page 107).

5 Turn to the right side and insert the cushion pad. Slipstitch the opening together firmly using double matching thread. (See Sewing Guide, page 108).

INTERLINED CURTAINS

Interlining your curtains is not essential unless they have an exceptionally long drop. In this case, the extra weight will help them to hang correctly. However, if you can afford the time and cost, interlining is well worth it for the excellent heat insulation and the feeling of luxurious thickness it will give your curtains. It also helps to reduce noise from the outside and to block out more light.

YOU WILL NEED

Curtain fabric
Cotton interlining – thick, fluffy bump or the less bulky domette
Lining sateen
Matching thread
Heading tape

To make

1 Estimate the amount of fabric needed and cut out the curtains and the lining sateen following the instructions on pages 13-14.

2 Join widths or half widths together where necessary, using a plain flat seam. Press open. There is no need to neaten the edges. Where a patterned fabric is used, pin the fabric together carefully, matching the pattern repeat and tack on the outside as in fig 34.

3 Cut out the interlining to the same size as the curtain lengths. Thick cotton bump and domette are loosely woven fabrics, so join them with a lapped seam using two rows of zigzag stitch.

4 Lay the curtain fabric on to the working surface with the right side down. Place the interlining on to the wrong side of the fabric, matching sides and lower edges. Then, fold the interlining back and lockstitch into position. Two rows of lockstitch should be worked to every width of fabric, stitching from the top to the bottom of the curtain length and preventing the interlining from falling away from the curtain fabric when it is hanging.

5 Turn in together 50mm (2in) of both curtain fabric and interlining at the side edges and along the lower edge. Tack and herringbone-stitch this into position (fig 35) and mitre the corners (see Sewing Guide, pages 108-9).

6 Lay the lining on top of the interlining and lockstitch into position thus locking the lining to the interlining. Trim the lining where necessary to make it the same size as the curtain (fig 36).

7 Fold in the lining 25mm (1in) at the sides and bottom of the curtain and tack. Do not mitre these corners. Slipstitch the lining into position as shown in fig 37.

8 Make a line of tacking across the curtain 15-20.5cm (6-8in) from the top edge to hold the lining and interlining in position while the heading tape is applied (fig 37).

9 Follow the instructions for applying heading tape on pages 14-15, press and hang.

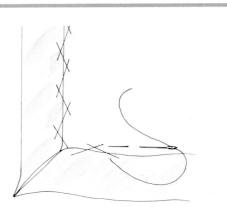

fig 35 Stitching sides and hem with herringbone

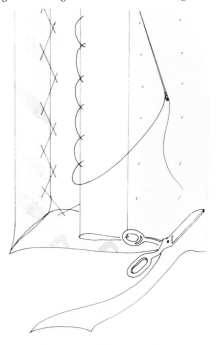

fig 36 Lockstitching and trimming the lining

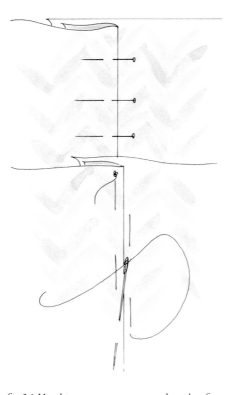

fig 34 Matching pattern repeats on lengths of fabric using outside tacking

fig 37 Tacking the three layers together for positioning the heading tape

BOLSTER CUSHIONS WITH PIPED SEAMS

Long bolster cushions are often used at the ends of sofas or at the head of a bed or divan. Covers can be made for them in combinations of many different fabrics but avoid those with a complex pattern as they can be difficult to match at the seams.

YOU WILL NEED

Bolster cushion pad
Furnishing fabric
Matching thread
Zip fastener measuring at least half the circumference of the cushion pad
Piping cord No 2 or 3
(boiled for 5 minutes and dried before use to ensure it will not shrink when cleaned)
Paper for pattern
Large round tray or plate
Zipper foot attachment for machine

To make

1 Measure the length and circumference of the bolster cushion adding 13mm (½in) allowance all round for turnings. Cut a piece of fabric to this size making sure it is on the straight grain (fig 38).

2 Make a paper pattern of the two circular end sections using a large round tray or plate as a guide and adding 13mm (½in) allowance all round for turnings. Cut two circles of fabric to the size required using the pattern.

3 With right sides facing, pin, tack and machine the long sides of the rectangle together. Leave an opening at the centre measuring at least half the circumference of the bolster cushion to allow the pad to be inserted easily (fig 39).

4 Insert a zip in the opening leaving equal hems on each side. Alternatively, the opening can be slipstitched together after the bolster pad has been inserted. This will depend to some degree on how often the bolster cover is likely to need cleaning.

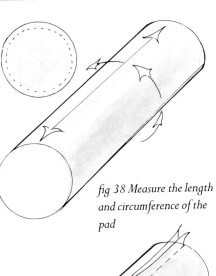

fig 38 Measure the length and circumference of the pad

fig 39 Stitch the side seam leaving a central opening

fig 40 Apply the piping to the end sections

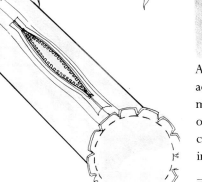

fig 41 The finished cover showing the clipped seams of the circular ends and the zip fastener

5 Prepare the bias strip and piping cord according to the instructions on page 109, then pin and tack to the two circular pieces of fabric. Clip the strip as it is applied so that it sits well and does not pucker (fig 40). (Alternatively, insert a frill instead of, or as well as, the piping cord. Full instructions for making frills are given on pages 23-4.)

6 Pin and tack the circular ends to the main body of the cover and clip the seam allowances. Machine into position using a zipper foot attachment and stitching as close as possible to the piping cord (fig 41).

7 Neaten the raw edges and turn the cover to the right side through the opening. Insert the cushion pad. If not using a zip fastener, sew up the opening firmly using slipstitch and strong matching thread.

DIVAN COVER

An ordinary single bed takes on new character when enhanced by a tailored cover made according to the instructions for an ottoman cover on page 57. With bolster cushions to match, the effect is of an inviting cosy sofa by day.

PLAIN SQUARE CUSHION

For full instructions see pages 23 and 24.

Traditional Comfort

PELMET FLOUNCE WITH LINED CURTAINS
LOOSE COVER FOR A SOFA
SQUARE FRILLED CUSHION
DROP-IN SEAT FOR DINING CHAIR
SKIRTED TABLECLOTH
ROUND TABLECLOTH
TABLE NAPKINS

It is possible to enjoy all the comfort and style of a traditional setting without it looking dull and old-fashioned or being difficult to maintain if you choose one of today's wide range of fabrics. Many are based on traditional designs, slightly modified to suit modern tastes and needs (lighter colours and smaller rooms for example), and are easier to clean which helps keep them looking fresh.

In this room a subtle greeny blue design with a pattern of leaves and flowers and the odd touch of coral pink makes an elegant companion to traditional style furniture in stripped pine. If you have a good feature, make sure you emphasize it. Here lovely large French windows have been shown to best advantage by framing them with a deep pleated pelmet of fabric and full floor-to-ceiling curtains. A three-seater sofa of classic shape has been fitted with loose covers in the same fabric, the deep sea-green cleverly picked out for the piping and to make a plain cloth for the circular table. This strong area of unadulterated colour has in turn been softened by a shorter, white lace-edged cloth to match those on the other tables — contrasting shapes and heights for added interest.

The coral pink of the fabric design makes the perfect accent colour and has been used here and there to bring the room to life: pink and white glass for the old-fashioned brass lamp and a pair of pretty frilled cushions in plain glazed chintz. Pink rosebud china and green napkins are the finishing touch for this smart but comfortable living room.

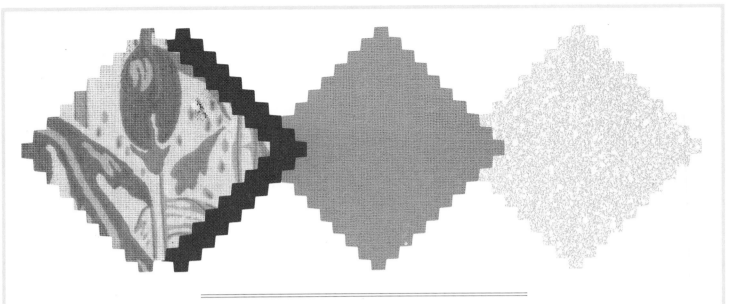

SAMPLES OF THE MATERIALS USED

1 Sofa covers, chair seat covers, curtains and pelmet
Machine-washable 100% cotton fabric in a cool greeny-blue leaf and coral pink flower pattern.

2 Piping and floor-length, circular tablecloth
Dry-cleanable, glazed 100% cotton chintz in deep sea-green.

3 Cushions
Dry-cleanable, glazed 100% cotton chintz in coral pink, the same shade as the poppies in the print.

4 Wallcovering
Scrubbable, ready-pasted vinyl wallpaper with a mottled finish.

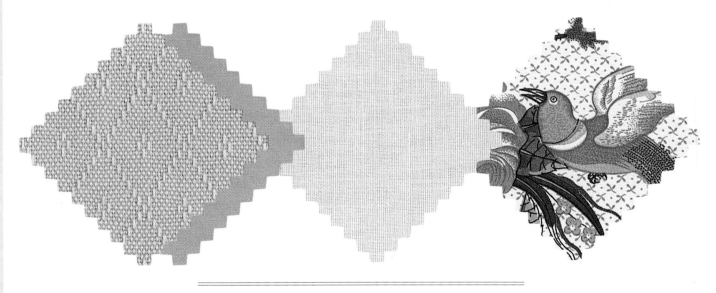

AN ALTERNATIVE COLOUR SCHEME

In a traditional room an important pattern in several soft colours can be successfully used on the walls if you keep the furnishings plain. Here a birds-and-flowers print in peach, cream and pale green spongeable wallpaper is combined with plain fabrics in the same colours. The tough 100% cotton fabric in a peach diamond weave is the perfect match and makes beautifully draped curtains and a fine shaped pelmet to show off the lovely window, and smart loose covers for the sofa. The shape of the sofa is emphasized with 100% glazed cotton peach chintz piping. Full-length circular tablecloths in the same fabric make the most of its pleasing sheen. Plain cream linen scatter cushions for the sofa are suitably restrained, but introduce a lighter tone. The secret with rooms composed in a traditional way is to strike the right balance between patterns and plains: however audacious the pattern you choose as your starting point, if you select all the plain colours from those it includes, resisting the temptation to introduce too many contrasts, the finished scheme will be sure to work.

PELMET FLOUNCES

Pelmet flounces, which are also known as valances, are a decorative feature which also serve a practical purpose. Like plain pelmets, they hide the curtain headings and conceal the tracks and fittings. They will also protect the tops of curtains from dirt and dust. At one time no window was thought complete without a pelmet flounce, but when an uncluttered look became more fashionable they fell into disuse. Now that a new generation of designers is appreciating the many uses of fabric in room settings they are enjoying a revival, not only as simple window headings, but as devices for varying the apparent size of a window.

Pelmet flounces are soft and informal in style. Make them gathered or pleated, using one of the commercial heading tapes; smocked and pencil-pleated headings or some of the more rigid curtain tapes now available are particularly suitable. Hang them from a special rail in front of the curtain track or attach them to a pelmet board above the curtain rail. Their use is not restricted to curtains; they are equally effective round dressing tables and vanity units or to decorate four-poster beds.

Pelmet flounces are made like miniature curtains and are best lined (except perhaps in kitchens and bathrooms). They can also be interlined with bump (a thick, fluffy cotton interlining) or stiffened with a self-adhesive or plain non-woven interfacing material. This gives the flounce body, and helps it to hang well.

Estimate the amount of fabric width needed for a pelmet flounce by measuring as for curtains. The depth of the flounce will depend on the length of the curtains. Allow 38mm (1½in) of flounce to each 30·5cm (12in) of curtain drop to make a rough estimate of the proportion suitable. Thus, on a 1·8m (2yd) length of curtain the valance should be approximately 23cm (9in) in depth. This is a helpful guide and can be varied to suit individual designs. From 18-30.5cm (7-12in) is average.

PELMET FLOUNCE WITH LINED CURTAINS

YOU WILL NEED

Curtain fabric
Matching thread
Curtain lining sateen
Cotton interlining (thick fluffy bump or the less bulky domette) or interfacing (self-adhesive bonded or non-woven to be stitched on)
Pleated heading tape and hooks
Rail or pelmet board with eyelet rings

To make

1 Cut out and make the lined curtains as on page 21. Only a simple standard pocketed tape is required for these as the curtain headings will be hidden underneath the flounce.

2 Cut out the fabric, lining and interlining, joining widths together if necessary. Match any pattern repeats carefully, using the outside tacking stitch (see Sewing Guide, page 107).

3 Make up the flounce as for an interlined curtain, turning in the two sides and lower hem 38mm (1½in). Trim the interlining to the exact size of the finished flounce at the side hems. Herringbone-stitch into position (see Sewing Guide, page 107).

4 Lockstitch the interlining and lining into position as shown in fig 42. Turn in the lining 25mm (1in) at the side and bottom hems and slipstitch all round.

5 Pin and tack the heading tape to the wrong side of the flounce, positioning it in such a way that the sets of pleats are evenly and correctly distributed on the right side of the flounce when they are drawn up as shown in the photograph.

6 When using a commercial tape that produces pleats automatically by pulling up cords, use a few stitches at the base of each set of pleats to secure it firmly in place. This gives a smarter finish (fig 43).

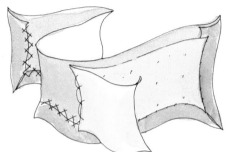

fig 42 Lockstitching the lining and interlining into position on the flounce

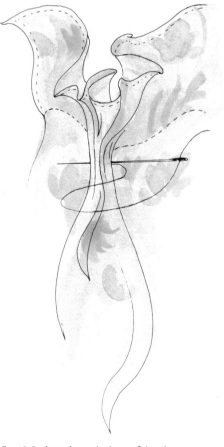

fig 43 Stabstitching the base of the pleat

fig 44 Positioning hooks in the tape

7 Place hooks in the tape (fig 44) and attach the flounce to the rail in front of the curtain track. If using a pelmet board, screw eyelet rings into it to match up with the hooks in the tape. Hook the flounce to the board using the eyelet rings (fig 45).

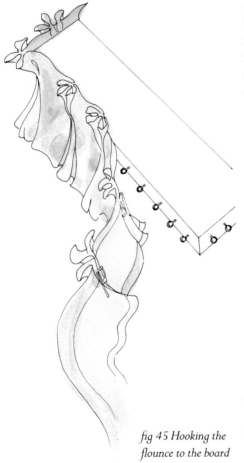

fig 45 Hooking the flounce to the board

LOOSE COVER FOR A SOFA

The same principles apply when preparing and making a cover for a sofa as for a chair. Check out the main guidelines on pages 15-16 before following the estimating and cutting-out procedures on page 22. More fabric is obviously needed for a sofa cover (from 10-15 metres/11-16½yds), which makes it more difficult to handle. More piping cord and bias strip are also required.

Make sure that the fabric is cut out with care, centring and matching any motifs so that they are the same on each seating unit. Motifs should also match on the seat or cushion covers. When making a three-seater loose cover cut the inside back in three sections, piping each seam. This makes the fabric easier to handle and helps it to mould well to the shape of the sofa.

Making frills
A gathered or pleated frill is often used on the bottom of a loose cover. They vary in depth from 15-20.5cm (6-8in) and should be made so that they finish 13mm (½in) from the floor. Allow 13mm (½in) turnings at the top of the frill and 25mm (1in) at the lower edge to make a 13mm (½in) double machined hem.

YOU WILL NEED

Furnishing fabric
Piping cord No 3
(boiled for 5 minutes and dried before use to
ensure it will not shrink when cleaned)
Matching thread
Paper for labelling sections
Tailor's chalk
Upholstery pins or skewers
Zipper foot attachment for machine

To make a gathered frill
1 Cut strips of fabric across the width of the fabric from selvedge to selvedge to the depth required plus turnings and hem allowance. If the strips have to be joined, make sure that the patterns are matched carefully (fig 46). This can be achieved most successfully by using the outside tacking stitch described on page 107

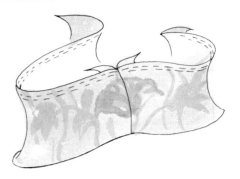

fig 46 Matching patterns when joining strips

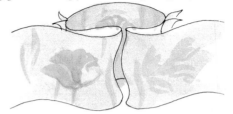

fig 47 Positioning seams in inverted pleats

(Sewing Guide). Where possible, position joins in the pleats at the sides or back of the cover.

2 Join the strips together with a 13mm (½in) flat seam and press open.

3 Turn up the hem 13mm (½in) and machine stitch.

4 In order to distribute the gathers evenly, divide the strip into four sections and work two rows of gathering stitches 13mm (½in) from the raw edge (fig 60).

5 Mark off four equal sections on the base line of the loose cover and pin the frill to the cover over the piping cord and bias strip, starting at the opening at the back seam. Draw up the gathering stitches and distribute the fullness evenly. Tack into position. Make two rows of machine stitching 6mm (¼in) apart using the zipper foot attachment and neaten the seam with a zigzag stitch.

Frill with inverted pleats
1 Cut out the strips of fabric as for the gathered frill but join the strips so that the seams are carefully positioned in the pleats where they will not show (fig 47). Several pleats can be made on a sofa cover as shown in fig 48.

fig 48 Positioning pleats on a sofa

fig 49, fig 50, fig 51 Making a tie-under finish

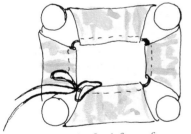

fig 52 A tie-under finish for a sofa

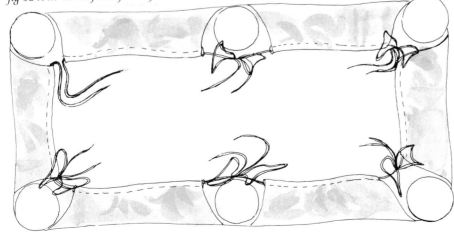

2 Turn up the hem 13mm (½in) and machine stitch.

3 Pin and tack the frill to the cover, starting at the back seam and making a half inverted pleat on each side of the opening. Make two rows of machine stitching and neaten the seam with a zig-zag stitch.

To make a tie-under finish
1 For a plain finish at the lower edge of a loose cover, cut out four strips of match-ing fabric approximately 15cm (6in) deep by the width of the outside back, outside arms and front sections.

2 Make a 13mm (½in) hem at the side of each strip, cutting them so that they fit round the legs of the chair or sofa. Make a casing along the bottom edge by turning up a 25mm (1in) double hem, through which to thread the tape or elastic (fig 49).

3 With right sides together, pin and tack the four strips into position as in fig 50, stitching them to the base line of the cover over the bias strip and piping cord. Machine stitch into position.

4 Thread a piece of strong tape or elastic through the casings and tie securely underneath the chair when the cover is in position (fig 51).

5 When making a tie-under finish for a sofa cover it is better to sew two 25.5cm (10in) tapes on to the strips and tie them together behind each leg (fig 52).

SQUARE FRILLED CUSHION

Square frilled cushions are made in the same way as round frilled cushions. Extra fullness is allowed at each corner so that the frill sits well. See page 24 for full instructions.

DROP-IN SEAT FOR DINING CHAIR

Dining chairs can be given a new lease of life or integrated into a new colour scheme by replacing their old seat covers. New material is stretched over the seat frame and tacked to the underside. Full instructions are given on page 98.

TABLECLOTHS

Tablecloths are both pretty and practical; they can protect valuable antique furniture from the hazards of day-to-day use, disguise the features of less elegant tables or provide a background for table settings in the dining room and kitchen. Small tables look attractive when draped to the floor and covered with a shorter cloth using a different fabric. They can be used for displaying favourite photographs and other decorative objects. Tablecloths for practical purposes should be made in easy-care fabrics that need little or no ironing. Alternatively, use fabrics that match or co-ordinate with other soft furnishings in your home. They can be lined and interlined as required, and trimmed with fringes, frills and ribbons to make them an original feature in living rooms and bedrooms (see fig 53). You can make attractive fitted table cloths for round, square or rectangular tables. For an elegant table-setting, any fabric left over from making a cloth for a dining table can be made up into matching napkins and place mats.

Protect polished surfaces from damage by first covering the table with a heat-resistant material made from latex rubber and cotton. Cut this to the exact size of the table and use it under the cloth. A glass top can be placed on top of the tablecloth to protect delicate fabrics.

Estimate the amount of fabric needed for square and rectangular tablecloths by measuring the table and allowing a generous overhang. Add to these measurements 25mm (1in) for seam allowances. Use the widest fabric possible to obviate the need for seams. If fabric has to be joined, match the pattern repeat carefully, using outside tacking (see Sewing Guide, page 107), and place the seam in the most inconspicuous place you can. Round tablecloths usually need to have joins made in the fabric in order to obtain the necessary width. Make joins on each side of a central panel so that they are as unobtrusive as possible as shown in fig 57.

SKIRTED TABLECLOTH

fig 53

YOU WILL NEED

Fabric
Matching thread
Paper for making pattern
Bias binding
Piping cord No 2
(boiled for 5 minutes and dried before use to
ensure it will not shrink when cleaned)
Zipper foot attachment for machine

To make

1 Cut out a paper pattern to the size of the table top (fig 54). Cut out the fabric to the pattern, allowing 13mm (½in) turnings. Apply bias strip and piping cord to the raw edge as for cushions (fig 20, page 23).

fig 54 Measuring the table

2 To estimate the amount of fabric needed for the skirt, measure from the table top to the floor and add 50mm (2in) for turnings. This will be the depth. For the width of the skirt measure the circumference of the table top and allow one and a half to twice this measurement (fig 54). Cut out the skirt section and join the short sides together to make a circle. Work two rows of gathering stitches 13mm (½in) from the top edge. Divide the skirt into equal sections if necessary, so that the gathers can be distributed evenly (fig 55).

fig 55 The skirt is divided into four equal sections so that the gathers can be drawn up evenly

3 With right sides together pin and tack the skirt to the top section of the cloth, drawing up the gathers and distributing them evenly. Machine stitch the seam using a zipper foot attachment if the edge has been piped. Neaten seams. Turn up a 13mm (½in) double hem, checking first that the tablecloth is the correct length. Alternatively, a frill can be applied to the lower edge of the cloth – the added weight will help the cloth to hang well. Make and attach this as in fig 22 on page 24 (*Round frilled cushion*). Adjust the depth of the skirt section accordingly.

TABLE NAPKINS

For full instructions see page 99.

3 Cut along the pencil line to obtain the paper pattern, then use it to cut out the fabric (fig 57). If the tablecloth is large, fold the square of fabric in four and use one quarter of the paper pattern only to cut out the fabric (fig 58).

4 Finish the raw edges of the tablecloth with a frill or other decorative trimming, making a narrow hem first, or bind the raw edges with bias binding. Notch the fabric all round as in fig 59 so that the hem sits well round the curved edge. Space the notches 25mm (1in) apart and cut them 13mm (½in) deep. Tack and machine stitch the bias binding to the raw edge. Trim seam to 6mm (¼in) and fold the binding to the wrong side of the cloth. Tack and hemstitch by hand (fig 60). Alternatively, the binding can be tacked and machine stitched to the hem as in figs 61 and 62.

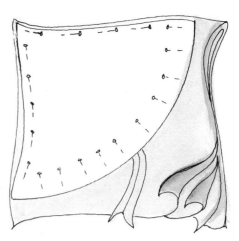

fig 58 Pinning the pattern for a large cloth

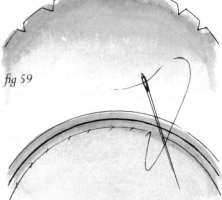

fig 59

ROUND TABLECLOTH

YOU WILL NEED

Fabric
Matching thread
Paper for making pattern
Pencil and string
Trimming or bias binding

To make

1 Measure across the top of the table to find its diameter, and down the side of the table to the point where the cloth will hang (fig 54). Double the side measurement and add the diameter to it to obtain the width of the finished tablecloth. You will need a square of fabric this size.

2 Make a paper pattern of a circle before cutting out the fabric. Take a large sheet of paper (brown paper is adequate – you can join it with adhesive tape if necessary) and then fold it in four so that each side is a little longer than the radius of the tablecloth. Attach a length of string firmly at the centre of the paper with a drawing pin, and tie a pencil at its loose end; then draw an arc on the paper from A to B keeping the pencil upright and the string tight (fig 56).

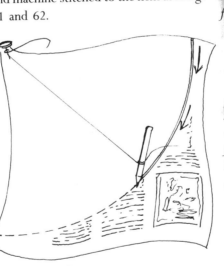

fig 56 Making the paper pattern

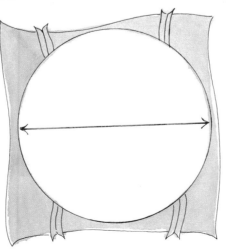

fig 57 Positioning the pattern on the fabric

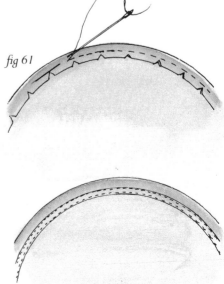

fig 60 Finishing the hem by hand. The bias binding is machine stitched to the raw edge then hemstitched by hand.

fig 61

fig 62 Finishing the hem by machine

Waking Up to Summer

THROW-OVER BEDSPREAD

PLAIN PILLOWCASE

FRILLED PILLOWCASE

GATHERED VALANCE

SCATTER CUSHIONS

PLEATED LAMPSHADE FROM CARD

SKIRTED TABLECLOTH

LINED CURTAINS WITH FRILL

The bedroom is perfect for creating the mood you want to wake up to every morning. The freshness of summer has been captured here in peach and aquamarine with a co-ordinated range of sprigs and stripes for curtains, covers and cloths. The beauty of matching and co-ordinated fabrics is that you can mix and match them for all kinds of accessories and know that they will look good. See how the en suite bathroom on pages 78-9 uses the same designs but in aquamarine with peach details — the combined effect is stunning.

This room has an unmistakably feminine touch with frilled curtains in a tiny sprigged material matched to a simple throw-over bedspread and a selection of scatter cushions in both the peach and aquamarine colourways. A clever detail is to pick out the peach colour in plain fabric for frills, edging and piping as well as a small throw-over cloth for the bedside table, and to make a pleated card lampshade to match.

An all-over tiny pattern lacks impact so a striped design from the same range has been introduced — peach and white with a thin aquamarine stripe which adds a smart new emphasis to the scheme. Used at floor level for a neat valance round the bed and on the diagonal for the floor-length tablecloth for added interest, it echoes the stripes of the soft bedside rug in shades of peach and beige. On the bed a large collection of scatter cushions mixing shapes, fabrics and frills introduces an interesting focal point that looks inviting and ties the whole design together.

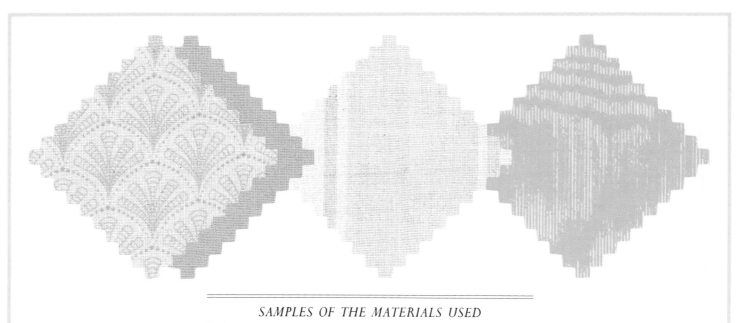

1 Bedspread, curtains and cushion covers
Peach, aquamarine and cream machine-washable 100% cotton in a
delicate sprig design.

3 Valance and long circular tablecloth
Peach, aquamarine and white Regency stripe in 100% washable cotton
echoes the colours of the main cotton print.

2 Small throw-over tablecloth, cushion frills, piping and bedspread edging
Machine-washable 100% cotton in peach.

4 Lampshade
Apricot wallpaper with a marbled effect.

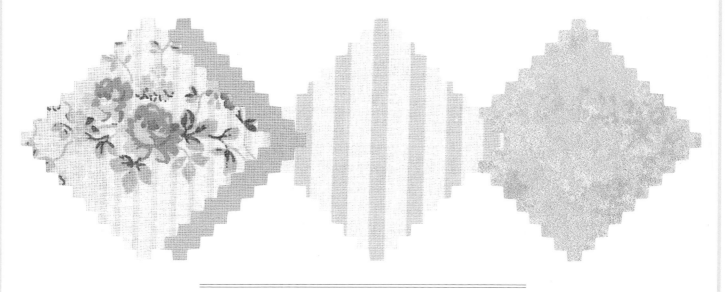

AN ALTERNATIVE COLOUR SCHEME

Replace peach and aquamarine with co-ordinating stripes and flowers in cool, clean pinks, blues and white, and the summery mood is still soft and feminine. Both the bedspread and curtains would look particularly pretty in an old-fashioned design of rambling roses and forget-me-nots against co-ordinating stripes and bands of colour. Pick out the pink and white candy stripe in the background to make the bed valance and floor-length cloth for the bedside table, using plain pink cotton for the smaller throw-over cloth. Make up an armful of frilled cushions in a combination of all three fabrics with pink frills to match the trimming on the bedcover. Pale blue marbled wallpaper picks out the blue of the flowered fabric perfectly, and, made into a pleated lampshade, strikes the right strong note in a predominantly pink and white scheme. It is the cool of the blue offsetting the warmth of the pink that makes this a balanced design, a touch of white adding crispness and clarity. This is why it is suited equally well to a cold, north-facing room as to a sunny, southerly aspect.

BEDCOVERS

Since bedspreads provide a large area of colour and texture they are often the focal point of a bedroom, especially a small one.

Bedspreads can be used over sheets and blankets or duvets and quilts to give a neat appearance to the bed during the daytime. Make them to match or co-ordinate with curtains, headboards and blinds choosing firm, medium-weight fabrics that do not crease easily and that wash or dry clean well. Remember that small and random match patterns are easier to handle and have less wastage from pattern matching than larger ones.

When estimating for fabrics be sure to take the measurements over a made-up bed with pillows and quilts in position (fig 63). Choose wide-width fabrics if possible to avoid joins in the fabric, but if these are necessary, place the width of fabric in the centre of the bedspread and make the joins at either side of it (fig 64). Make sure that pattern repeats are carefully matched, using outside tacking for greatest accuracy (see Sewing Guide, page 107).

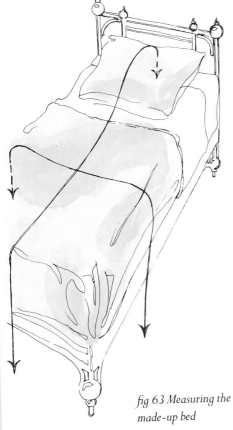

fig 63 Measuring the made-up bed

THROW-OVER BEDSPREAD

This style of bedspread is usually allowed to fall to the floor at the sides and foot of the bed unless it is used over a valance which fits over the base of the bed and underneath the mattress. In this case, make the bedspread to fall just below the top of the valance, for which identical or co-ordinating fabric should be used.

YOU WILL NEED

Fabric (approx. 6m (6½yds) of 120cm (48in) wide plain fabric for a single or medium-sized double bed; allow more fabric for frills, piping, binding and if using patterned fabric)
Matching thread
Lining (optional)
Large tray or plate

To make

1 To estimate for fabric requirements decide where the bedspread will hang and take measurements over the made-up bed. Allow enough fabric to tuck underneath the pillows (approx. 15cm (6in)).

2 Cut two widths of fabric the length required and cut off all selvedges. Use one width for the centre of the bedspread and cut the other width in half lengthwise. Join these pieces to the centre panel matching pattern repeats carefully (fig 64). If you are lining the bedspread, use flat seams and press them open. Neaten the edges with a zigzag stitch. If not lining, join the fabric with a French seam or a flat fell seam. Trim off the fabric at either side if necessary to reduce the width to the required size.

3 Turn in 13mm (½in) double hems all round the bedspread and mitre square corners. Tack and machine into position. The foot of the bedspread can be rounded at the corners by using a large tray or plate to draw the curved shape. Cut the fabric and fold the bedspread in half, cutting the other side to match. Notch curved shapes when making the hem, to take in excess fullness (fig 65).

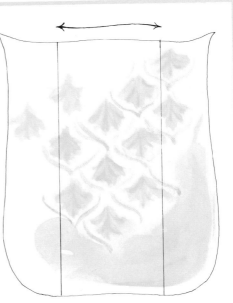

fig 64 The full width of fabric is placed at the centre and extra width is joined at the sides

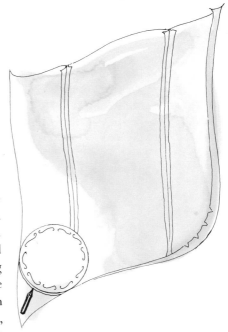

fig 65 Making the rounded corners

4 To make a lining for a throw-over bedspread, cut out the lining fabric and join the seams so that they match those on the cover fabric. Lay the face fabric out flat and place the lining in position, wrong sides together. Match the seams and lock-stitch the lining to the face fabric along the seams. Trim off the lining to the exact size of the bedspread. Turn in 25mm (1in) all round and tack and slipstitch into position (see instructions for lined curtains, page 21).

5 Add more weight and interest by sandwiching a thin layer of synthetic wadding between two pieces of co-ordinating fabrics. Work rows of machine stitching 50-75mm (2-3in) apart, marking out lines from the centre of the bedspread using tailor's chalk or long tacking stitches (fig 66). Quilt the bedspread on the machine using a long straight stitch. If available, use a quilting gauge to ensure equal distances between the lines of stitching. Trim the raw edges and tack round the outside edge of the bedspread 25mm (1in) from the edge. Cut a strip of bias binding 75mm (3in) wide from matching or contrasting fabric and apply this to the edge of the bedspread on the right side. Tack and machine into position. Fold over to the wrong side, turning in 13mm (½in) and tack and slipstitch along the machine stitch line (fig 67).

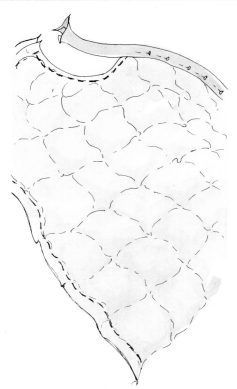

fig 67 Binding the raw edges

6 Alternatively, the edges of a bedspread can be finished with a frill or other decorative trimming (as shown in fig 68).

fig 66 Quilting the bedcover

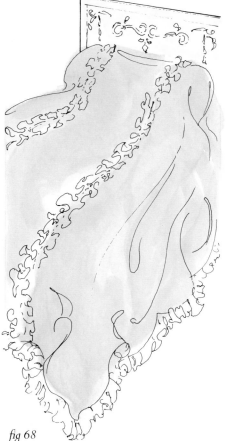

fig 68

PILLOWCASES

Make plain or frilled pillowcases to match or co-ordinate with duvet covers and sheets, choosing polyester/cotton sheeting for ease of care. These fabrics are obtainable in wide widths, thus avoiding the need for too many seams. As pillowcases are washed frequently, use French seams where possible since these enclose all the raw edges and prevent fraying.

Pillows are made in rectangular or square shapes and vary in size according to their filling, so measure them carefully before cutting out the fabric.

PLAIN PILLOWCASE

YOU WILL NEED

For a pillow 51×76cm (20×30in) a strip of fabric 53.5×173cm (21×68in)
Matching thread

To make

1 Measure the pillow, being generous with the measurements as the cover should not constrict the filling. Allow 13mm (½in) turnings.

2 For a pillow measuring 51×76cm (20×30in) cut a strip of fabric 53·5×173cm (21in×68in) (or cut it in separate sections if this works out more economically with the fabric available).

3 Fold a 13mm (½in) double hem along one short side and on the other turn over first 6mm (¼in) and then 25mm (1in) to make a hem. Machine stitch hems.

4 Fold the fabric as in fig 69, folding in the side with the narrow hem for 15cm (6in) and having the right sides of the pillowcase outside. Pin, tack and machine stitch, allowing 13mm (½in) turnings. Trim seams to 3mm (⅛in) and turn to the wrong side (fig 70).

5 Complete the French seam by tacking and machining round the three sides; turn the pillowcase to the right side and press.

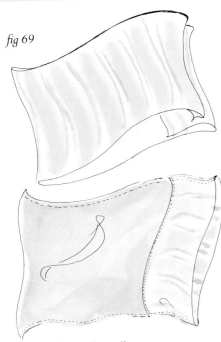

fig 69

of the flap section. Tack and machine stitch.

2 Turn in 6mm (¼in) and then 38mm (1½in) to make a hem on one short side of the back section. Tack and machine stitch.

3 Cut out and prepare a double frill (fig 71) following the instructions on pages 23-4 (*Round frilled cushion*). For a 50mm (2in) wide double frill, cut a strip of fabric on the straight grain 12·5cm (5in) wide by one and a half to twice the measurement round the pillow.

4 Join the short edges of the strip together with a 13mm (½in) flat seam and press open.

fig 71 Making a double frill

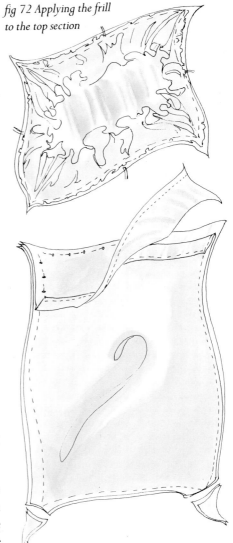

5 Fold the fabric in half lengthwise and mark it into quarters using tailor's chalk. Work two rows of gathering stitches in each section 6-13mm (¼-½in) from the raw edges, taking the stitches through both layers of fabric.

fig 72 Applying the frill
to the top section

fig 70 Making a plain pillowcase

FRILLED PILLOWCASE

YOU WILL NEED

Sheeting fabric for pillowcase
Frill – make the frill from matching or co-ordinating fabric, or choose a ready-made trimming
Matching thread
Tailor's chalk

To make

1 For a 51×76cm (20×30in) pillow cut out three sections for the pillowcase with measurments as for plain pillowcase (see page 44 opposite for instructions), making a 6mm (¼in) hem along one long side

6 Divide the front section of the pillowcase into four equal sections and mark with tailor's chalk.

7 Pin and tack the frill to the top section with right sides together. Distribute the gathers evenly, but allowing a little extra fullness at each corner (fig 72). This extra fabric will ensure that the frill stands out properly.

8 With the right sides together pin and tack the front section to the back section. The back section should be positioned 13mm (½in) from the raw edge of the front section (fig 73).

9 Pin and tack the right side of the flap to the wrong side of the back section taking 13mm (½in) turnings (fig 73).

10 Machine round the four sides of the pillowcase. Clip the corners and neaten the seams and turn the pillowcase through the flap opening to the right side (fig 73).

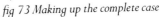

fig 73 Making up the complete case

VALANCE

A valance fits over the base of the bed and underneath the mattress. It hides the bed legs and storage space, and protects the base from dust (fig 74).

Choose fabrics that are 'easy care' and do not crease, or match them to other soft-furnishing fabrics that co-ordinate with headboard covers, duvets and bed-covers. Polyester/cotton sheeting washes well and the whole of the valance can be made from this fabric. If using furnishing fabrics use calico (or sheeting) to make the base section as this is less costly.

A valance can be gathered or pleated, and the amount of fabric needed depends on the style chosen and the size of the bed; 4·5 metres (5yds) of 120cm (48in) wide fabric is usually sufficient for a single-size bed whichever style is chosen, but check requirements by measuring first (fig 75) as bed bases are often of different heights. For a gathered frill allow one and a half to twice the measurement round the bed by the height of the base plus 75mm (3in) for turning allowance. For an inverted pleat at each corner of the foot of the bed allow the measurement round the bed plus 40·5cm (16in) for each pleat by the height of the base, plus 75mm (3in) for turnings. For an equal-space/equal-pleat finish allow twice the measurement round the bed by the height of the base, plus 75mm (3in) for turnings.

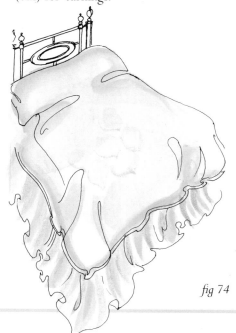

fig 74

fig 75 Measuring the bed for a valance

GATHERED VALANCE

YOU WILL NEED

Furnishing fabric (or sheeting)
(approx. 4·5m (5yds) for a single bed)
Matching thread
Calico
Piping cord No 3
(boiled for 5 minutes and dried before use to ensure it will not shrink when cleaned)
Tailor's chalk
Bias strip

To make

1 Cut out the base section of the valance from calico or sheeting, cutting it to the size of the top of the base and allowing 25mm (1in) all round for turnings.

2 Make a 13mm (½in) hem all round the base section and machine stitch into position. Measure and mark this into six equal sections using tailor's chalk or tailor's tacks (fig 76).

3 Cut out three strips of fabric 15cm (6in) wide for the facings. Two must be the

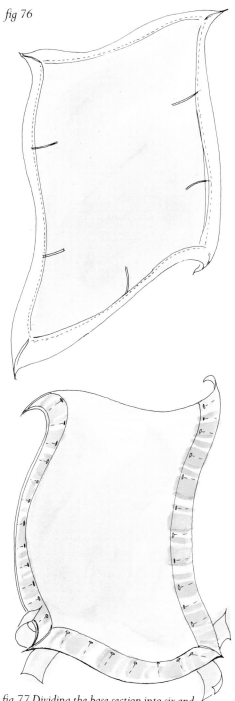

fig 76

fig 77 Dividing the base section into six and applying the facings

length of the bed and one its width, plus 25mm (1in) turning allowance. Pin the facings to the base section in order to mitre the two corners (fig 77). Remove the pins, take the facings off the base section and machine stitch the mitred corners in position leaving 13mm (½in) unstitched at each end. Fold in the raw edges of the facing sections 13mm (½in) and press (fig 78).

6 For the piped edge cut enough bias strip 38mm (1½in) wide to fit round the base of the bed. (Use the quick method on pages 109-10, Sewing Guide.) Pin and tack the bias strip and the piping cord over the gathered edge of the frill (fig 80).

7 Pin the right side of the facing to the right side of the frill over the piping and along the fold line of the facing. Position the mitred corners at the foot of the valance. Tack and machine stitch into position and trim seams to 13mm (½in).

8 Position the valance on the base of the bed and pin and tack the facing to the right side of the base section along the fold line. Machine stitch into position, using a large zigzag stitch to prevent the facing from puckering (fig 81).

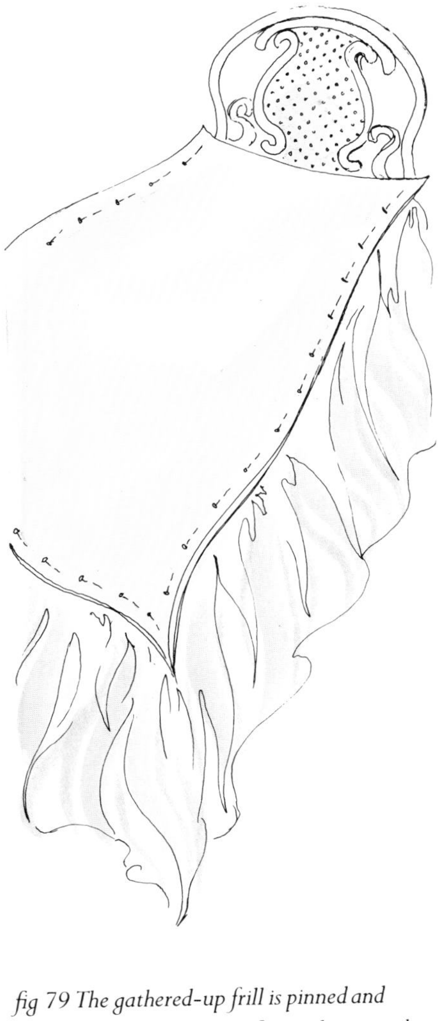

fig 80 Pinning the bias strip and piping cord over the gathered edge of the frill

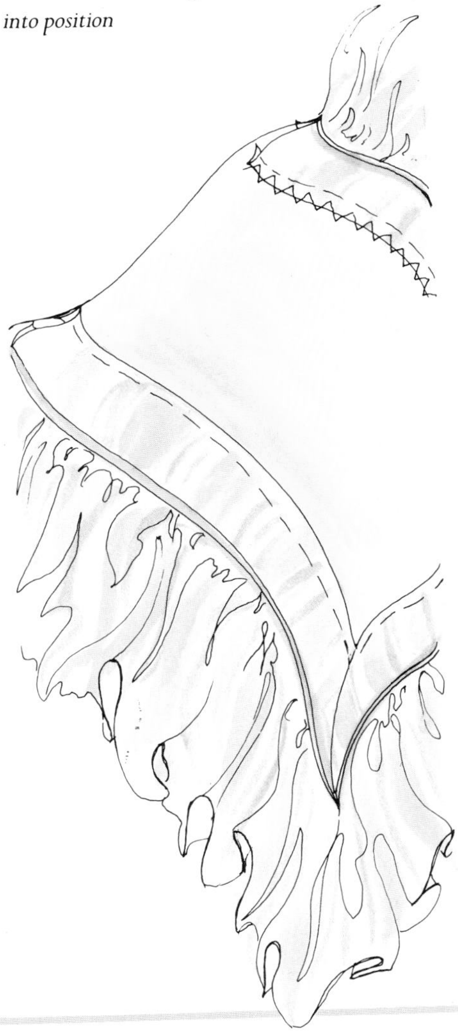

fig 81 Tacking the facing to the base section to enclose all the raw edges, and machine stitching into position

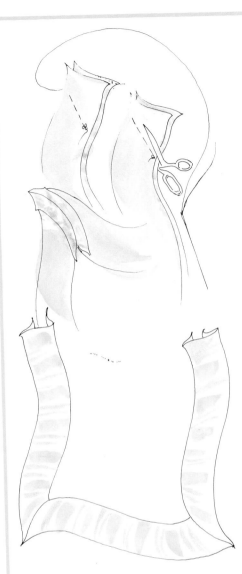

fig 78 Stitching, trimming and pressing the facings to form a mitred corner

4 Cut out strips of face fabric for the frill, joining if necessary to obtain the required length. Make a 13mm (½in) double hem at the ends of the frill and along the lower edge.

5 Divide and mark the frill into six equal sections and work two rows of gathering stitches between each mark, 13mm (½in) from the raw edge. With right sides outside, draw up the gathering stitches so that they fit into each section marked on the base section, (fig 76) taking care to distribute the gathers evenly. Pin and tack the frill to the base section with the right sides outside, fitting the valance on the base of the bed as you work (fig 79).

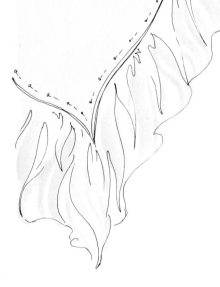

fig 79 The gathered-up frill is pinned and tacked to the base section of the valance, with right sides outside, distributing the gathers evenly

SCATTER CUSHIONS

Small cushions are an attractive way of decorating a bed. For the most sumptuous effect, make a selection of shapes in lightweight furnishings or dress fabrics such as satin, lace or broderie Anglaise and trim them with plenty of frills or other decorative edgings. They can often be made up from remnants of fabric left over from other projects, and can co-ordinate or contrast with your main colour scheme.

Use a ready-made pad, or make one yourself, filling it with loose synthetic wadding mixed with pot pourri or dried lavender. Instructions are given here for a heart shape but other shapes can be made just as easily following the same principles.

Instructions are given on page 24 for making a round frilled cushion, a square frilled cushion and a plain square cushion, and suitable materials for cushion pad fillings are described in the Introduction, page 17.

HEART-SHAPED CUSHION

YOU WILL NEED

Fabric for cushion cover
Matching thread
Frill or decorative trimmings
Lavender, pot pourri or other dried
sweet-smelling herbs
Paper to make pattern
Fabric for cushion pad – choose calico or cotton
lawn
Loose synthetic filling

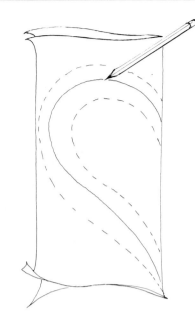

fig 82 *Making a heart-shaped pattern*

fig 83 *Stitching the pad cover*

fig 84 *Applying trimming to the cover*

To make

1 Make a pattern of the heart shape by folding a sheet of paper in half lengthwise and drawing on to it one side of a heart as in fig 82. Adjust the pattern if a larger or a smaller size is required. Remember that when the filling is inserted the shape will become smaller. Allow 13mm (½in) turning allowances.

2 Using the paper pattern, cut out the fabric for the inner pad, and make it up, placing the right sides together.

3 Pin, tack and machine all round the fabric leaving an opening along one side (fig 83). Clip seams and turn to the right side.

4 Fill with loose synthetic wadding mixed with sweet-smelling dried herbs or lavender, making sure that these are sufficiently covered by the filling so that they do not show through when the cushion is finished. Slipstitch the opening together.

5 Measure the cushion pad and estimate the amount of cover fabric needed. Cut this to the size required using the paper pattern. Allow 13mm (½in) turnings all round.

6 Apply trimming or lace to the right side of the top section of the cushion cover, or decorate with other surface embroidery (fig 84).

7 Make a frill or apply lace or other trimming to the outer edge of the cushion, pinning and tacking into position with gathers evenly distributed (see pages 23-4, *Round frilled cushion*). Allow extra fabric at each corner so the frill sits well.

8 With right sides facing, pin and tack the back section to the front section, leaving an opening along one side of the cushion through which to insert the cushion pad. Machine carefully into position.

9 Insert the cushion pad and slipstitch the opening firmly together.

PLEATED LAMPSHADE FROM CARD

You can make a firm lampshade using either wallpaper or card. Alternatively, bond fabric on to special PVC shade material to make a more lasting shade by pressing the fabric on to its sticky surface and tearing away the protective backing.

Choose a conical strutted frame coated with plastic to protect it from rusting, and avoid the need for taping.

Estimate the amount of paper or fabric needed by measuring the circumference of the bottom ring of the frame. The material can be joined if necessary to give the required length. The depth should be the height of the side strut plus 50mm (2in) (to allow for an overlap of 25m (1in) at both the top and bottom rings).

YOU WILL NEED

Strutted conical lampshade frame
Paper, card, or fabric and PVC backing material
A hole punch
Clear-drying adhesive
A length of cord or narrow ribbon

To make

1 Cut out the paper to the required size. If joins have to be made do not make them until the pleating is worked, then conceal them in a pleat.

2 Mark out guide lines for pleating on the wrong side of the paper using a faint pencil line (fig 85). Pleats measuring 19mm (¾in) are effective, but they can be varied to suit the size of the shade.

3 Neatly fold the paper into concertina-like pleats using the guide lines on the wrong side (fig 85). Make joins if necessary by overlapping the ends of the paper and securing with a clear-drying adhesive. Let this dry thoroughly. Finish the pleating by overlapping and glueing into position.

4 Punch a hole in the middle of each pleat using the guide line (fig 85) and thread a length of cord or ribbon through the holes to draw up the pleating to fit the top ring of the frame (fig 86).

5 Arrange the pleats carefully on the frame and tie with a bow (fig 87). If necessary the shade can be secured to the frame more firmly by stitching a length of thread round the cord and the top ring (fig 88).

6 No trimming is needed to complete this type of shade.

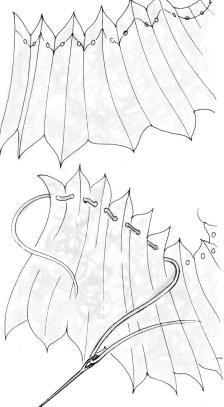

fig 85 Folding the paper according to the guide lines

fig 86 Threading cord or ribbon through the punched holes

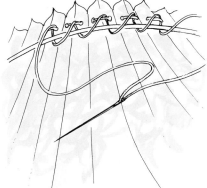

fig 87 Arranging the pleats and tying firmly with a bow

fig 88 Stitching the shade to the top ring of the frame

SKIRTED TABLECLOTH

Full instructions for making a skirted tablecloth are given on page 38.

LINED CURTAINS WITH FRILL

For full instructions see page 82.

The Tailored Touch

TAILORED BEDCOVER WITH PIPING
AND PILLOW GUSSET

BOXED CUSHIONS FOR HEADBOARD

PELMET

OTTOMAN COVER

LINED CURTAINS WITH HEADING TAPE

*Made-to-measure soft furnishings crisply tailored and finished in
contrasting or co-ordinating trimmings will always look sleek and smart,
making them ideally suited to more masculine taste or anyone who
dislikes fuss and frills.*

*This cool grey bedroom has been highlighted in bright
pillar-box red and furnished with black and shiny chrome to create a
room that is both dramatic and dignified. Height and weight is provided
by floor-length grey curtains hidden behind a deep matching pelmet, its
sculptured shape outlined in red, a long thin chrome cupboard and a
series of tall, black-framed posters that echo the art deco feel
of the furniture.*

*The red and grey theme of the pelmet is picked up
in the bedcover made in matching grey lozenge fabric piped in scarlet.
The cover has been cleverly pleated and tailored for smart, well-defined
shaping and includes a proper pillow gusset to ensure a good fit. For extra
comfort and impact, the traditional padded headboard has been replaced
by boxed cushions hung from a chrome pole. An ottoman at the foot of
the bed is fitted with a box-pleated red and grey cover to match.*

*A bright red cushion and angular metal folding chair
picks up on the piping round the covers and adds just the right amount of
colour and excitement, while an extra note of drama is provided by a
modern alternative to the chaise-longue — a moody reclining chair in
black leather and chrome.*

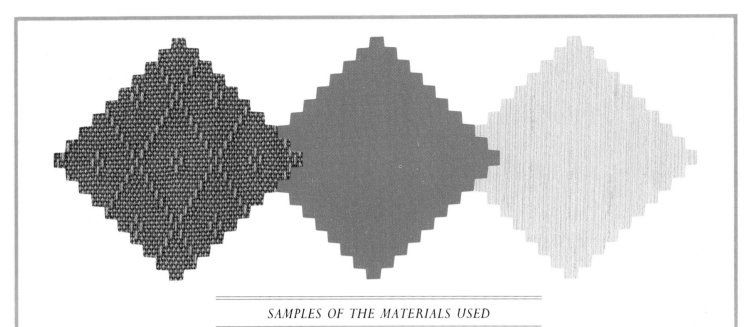

SAMPLES OF THE MATERIALS USED

1 Curtains, pelmet, bedspread and headboard, ottoman covers
Heavyweight, upholstery fabric in a grey diamond-weave 100% cotton.

2 Piping
Dry-cleanable, glazed 100% cotton chintz in pillar-box red.

3 Wallcovering

Fully washable, pale grey wallpaper with a textured finish provides the best background for a scheme which depends on simplicity for success. Pattern on the walls would detract from the clarity of tailored lines.

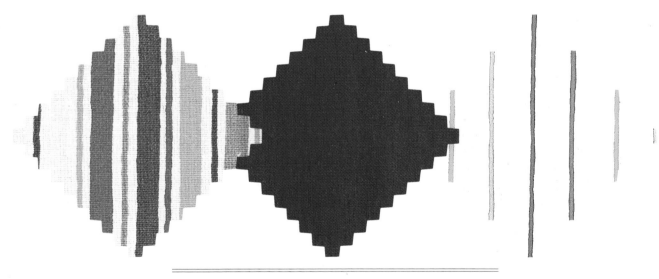

AN ALTERNATIVE COLOUR SCHEME

The smart tailored look is admirably suited to bold striped fabrics as well as plain ones. Substitute a striking coloured-stripe design on cream for the sophisticated plain greys and scarlet and this bedroom immediately takes on a younger, more light-hearted atmosphere. A washable cream wallpaper with thin stripes of burgundy, grey, navy and orange would echo the slick chrome lines of the furniture and maintain the feeling of height and dignity in the room. Ideally it should be matched to a co-ordinating fabric with wider stripes in exactly the same colours for a pair of dramatic floor-length curtains and a shaped pelmet to carry that feeling on round the room. The fabric is washable 100% cotton which makes it equally suitable for a tailored bedcover with matching ottoman and boxed bedhead cushions, all piped and trimmed in a deep blue cotton chintz which helps anchor this rather bold design and accentuate the tailored effect of the furnishings. Deep colours used in positive patterns need not be overpowering as long as they are counterbalanced by a neutral background such as cream or a shade of white, and the discriminating addition of a plain colour to bind the design together.

TAILORED BEDCOVER WITH PIPING AND PILLOW GUSSET

This bedspread is made to fit the bed with a pillow gusset designed to tuck over and behind the pillow for a smart tailored appearance. An extra piece of fabric inserted at the head of the bed allows the bedspread to go over the pillows without lifting it off the ground (fig 89). Its size will depend on the size and number of pillows; a standard pillow measuring 50×74cm (19×29in) will need a finished gusset 50-51cm (20in) long and a height of 12.5cm (5in) for a single pillow, 25.5cm (10in) for two.

YOU WILL NEED

Fabric
Matching thread
Lining sateen
Interfacing (iron-on bonded type or non-woven)
Paper for pattern
Piping cord No 3
(boiled for 5 minutes and dried before use to ensure it will not shrink when cleaned)
Trimming (optional)

To make

1 Measure the bed as in fig 90 allowing 25mm (1in) for turnings and approximately 30·5cm (12in) extra on the length to allow for the height of the pillows and the tuck-away behind them.

2 Cut out and join the fabric widths if necessary to make the central section of the bedcover. Match pattern repeats carefully using outside tacking (see page 107, Sewing Guide).

3 Make a paper pattern of the gusset to fit your individual pillow requirements. From this cut out two pillow gussets, one for the left, one for the right, taking care to match any pattern on the fabric.

4 From the same pattern cut two pieces of interlining which will help the gusset keep its shape. Tack or iron the interfacing to the wrong side of the gusset.

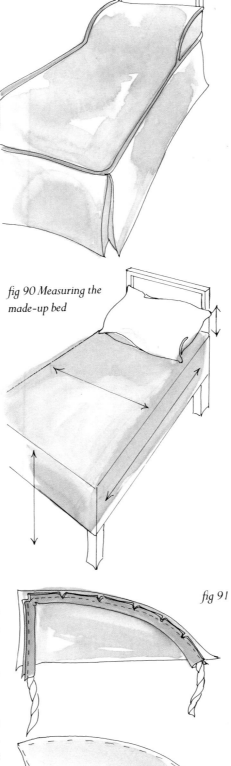

fig 89

fig 90 Measuring the made-up bed

fig 91

fig 92 Apply the piping and attach the gusset to the main section

5 Cut and prepare enough bias strips and piping cord to fit round the bed and gusset using the quick method on pages 109-10 (Sewing Guide).

6 Pin and tack the piping along the top and back edges of the gusset. Clip the curves and machine stitch (fig 91).

7 Pin the pillow gusset to the central section of the bedcover, allowing a 50mm (2in) allowance for a hem at the top edge (fig 92). Machine stitch.

8 Pin and tack the piping to the central section of the bedcover, starting at the back of one pillow gusset and continuing round to the back of the other. Machine stitch.

9 Cut out strips of fabric for the frill, allowing 40·5cm (16in) for each inverted pleat at the foot. Join if necessary to obtain the required length. If possible, position seams so that they are hidden in a pleat. Make a 13mm (½in) double hem along the lower edge of the frill.

10 Apply a trimming if you wish, along the lower edge 50-75mm (2-3in) above the hem, making a guide line with tacking stitches. Use small running stitches and matching thread, taking care not to pull the stitches too tightly or the trimming will pucker.

11 With right sides together, pin and tack the frill over the piping cord to the central section. Make an inverted pleat at each corner at the foot of the bedspread. Machine stitch in position. Cut across the corners (fig 93), trim and neaten seams.

To line the bedcover

12 Use the gusset pattern and cover measurements to cut out the pieces of lining sateen.

13 With right sides together, join the short back edge of the pillow gusset lining to the central section lining, leaving 50mm (2in) for turnings at the top of the central section.

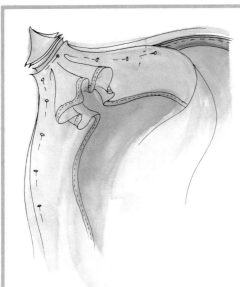

fig 93 Making an inverted pleat at the corner

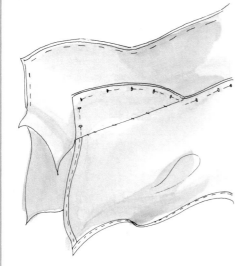

fig 94 Pinning the lining to the cover

14 Lay the lining to the wrong side of the bedcover, matching seams. Fold back the lining to each seam and lockstitch into position on the seams. Tack the lining in position approximately 10cm (4in) from the piped edge.

15 Pin the long straight edge of the pillow gusset lining to the frill, turning in 13mm (½in) and enclosing the raw edges (fig 94). Tack and hem.

16 Pin and tack the curved edge of the pillow gusset lining to the matching seam of the bedspread (fig 94). Machine stitch.

17 Turn under the lining round the two sides and bottom, tack and hem.

BEDHEADS

Boxed cushions fixed to the wall make effective bedheads and are inexpensive to make using rigid plastic or latex foam blocks for the foundation. Have the foam cut to the size required, or cut it yourself using a very sharp knife. Cover the blocks with calico, ticking or cotton lining sateen before making the outer cover.

Box cushions are square or rectangular and are made from two pieces of fabric with a welt or border all round. Make this from four separate strips of fabric to ensure a good fit.

Cushions can match or co-ordinate with bedcovers and valances and their smart, tailored appearance looks good in a masculine bedroom or a bed-sitting room. Hang them from curtain poles above divans to make backrests, or tie them to existing headboards for extra comfort.

Openings on box cushions must be large enough to insert the rigid pad easily and should therefore extend round the sides of the cover approximately 10cm (4in) or the width of the welt (fig 95).

BOXED CUSHIONS FOR HEADBOARD

YOU WILL NEED

Fabric for cushion cover
Matching thread
Cushion pad
Piping cord No 3
(boiled for 5 minutes and dried to ensure it will not shrink when cleaned)
(allow twice the measurement round the outside of the pad)
Zipper foot attachment for machine

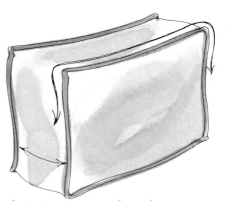

fig 95 The opening on a box cushion

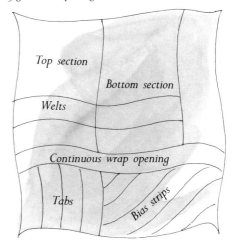

fig 96 Cutting plan for boxed cushion

To make

1 Measure the pad and make a plan as in fig 96 to estimate the amount of fabric needed. If the pad is a rigid one exact measurements must be taken, and to these must be added 13mm (½in) turning allowances. Allow a little more if the fabric frays easily, and neaten all raw edges before making up the cushion.

2 Cut out the fabric and tack the top and bottom sections together in the centre (with right sides facing) to hold them together. Pin each welt in separately to the right side of the top and bottom sections (fig 97) and tack them 25mm (1in) from all the raw edges so that the bias strip and piping cord can be inserted in the space between the tacking stitches and the raw edges.

3 Pin, tack and machine stitch the welts together at all four corners, leaving 13mm (½in) unstitched at each end (fig 98). Press these seams open.

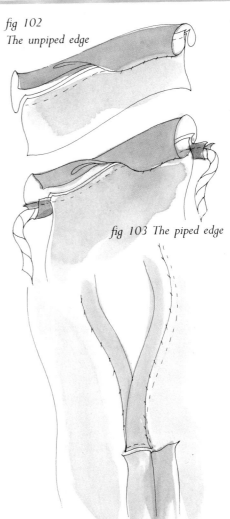

fig 102
The unpiped edge

fig 103 The piped edge

fig 97 Tacking the top and
bottom sections together,
and pinning the first welt

fig 98 Pinning the
welts in position

4 Cut and prepare the bias strips and the piping cord (using the quick method described on pages 109-10, Sewing Guide). Pin and tack this to the top and bottom sections of the cover and the welt, clipping corners (fig 99). Machine stitch round the top section using a zipper foot attachment to enable the stitches to be positioned close to the cord. (Do not machine the bottom section until the loops have been inserted.)

5 Prepare two loops for the cushion, making them long enough to hang round the curtain pole, usually from 30·5-38cm (12-15in). Cut two strips of fabric on the straight grain 15cm (6in) wide and fold them in half lengthwise. Make a 13mm (½in) flat seam and press open, positioning the seam at the back of the loop.

6 Mark the positions for the loops on the bottom section of the cushion cover. Unpick the tacking stitches and insert the loops between the top and bottom sections. Pin and tack them in position on top of the piping cord. Re-tack the seam. Mark the position for the opening along the back and side edges and machine stitch all round the bottom section leaving the opening unstitched. Remove all tacking stitches and turn the cover to the right side.

7 Finish the opening with a continuous wrap, or slipstitch the opening together after the cushion pad has been inserted.

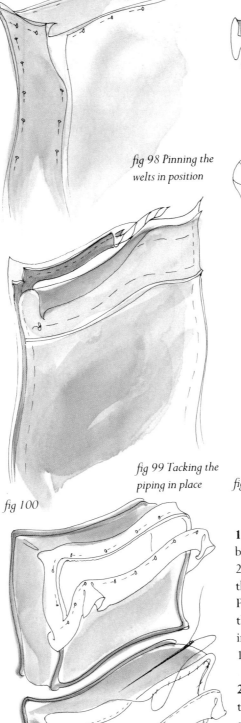

fig 99 Tacking the
piping in place

fig 100

fig 101 Making the
continuous wrap

fig 104 Finishing off the opening

To make a continuous wrap opening
1 Cut a strip of fabric 64mm (2½in) wide by twice the length of the opening plus 25mm (1in) for turnings. Join the strip at the short sides by a 13mm (½in) flat seam. Pin and tack the right side of the strip to the right side of the cushion cover opening, taking 13mm (½in) turnings (fig 100). Machine stitch.

2 Cut away 13mm (½in) from the strip on the unpiped edge. Turn in 13mm (½in) and hemstitch to the wrong side of the opening to make a facing (figs 101, 102).

3 On the other side of the opening fold over 13mm (½in) to make a strap and then hemstitch to the stitching line (fig 103). Hand stitch across both ends of the opening as in fig 104, and sew hooks or snap fasteners to the strap and the facing.

PELMET

YOU WILL NEED

Face fabric
Cotton interlining (thick, woolly bump or the
less bulky domette)
Matching thread
Pelmet buckram
Curtain lining sateen
Trimming (optional)
Heading tape or touch-and-close fastening tape
Paper to make pattern

To make

1 To estimate the materials needed, measure the pelmet board including the returns at each end (these should normally be approximately 10cm (4in) deep to accommodate the curtains and their track underneath). Add 5cm (2in) for turnings. The depth of the pelmet should be determined by the length of the curtains – allow 38mm (1½in) of pelmet per 30·5cm (12in) of curtain drop (or one sixth of floor-length curtains). This is a guide only and can be adapted to suit the treatment of the individual window. To this measurement add 10cm (4in) for turnings.

fig 105 Making the paper pattern

2 Fold a sheet of paper the length of the board plus returns in half lengthwise. Draw a design for half of the pelmet (fig 105). Cut out the pelmet buckram.

3 Cut a piece of face fabric 10cm (4in) larger all round than the size of the buckram. Centre a fabric width in the middle of the pelmet and join extra fabric if necessary at the side edges. Match pattern repeats carefully.

4 Cut the interlining 50mm (2in) larger all round than the size of the buckram shape, joining it if necessary with a lapped seam and a zigzag stitch.

5 Lay the buckram shape on to the interlining fabric. Dampen it slightly round the edge with a cloth and fold over the interlining 25mm (1in) a little at a time. Press with a hot iron to make the interlining adhere to the buckram (fig 106). Slash curves where necessary and cut away surplus interlining fabric at right-angled curves to help the material lay properly.

6 Lay the pelmet shape on to the wrong side of the face fabric. Dampen the buckram at the edges and apply the fabric as for the interlining. Mitre each corner and slipstitch. Reinforce slashes with a few buttonhole stitches (fig 107).

7 Apply trimming at this stage if used, fixing it to the right side of the pelmet.

8 Cut a strip of curtain lining sateen 50mm (2in) larger all round than the pelmet shape. Turn in 13mm (½in) along the top edge and press. Apply to the wrong side of the pelmet, pinning and slipstitching into position. Cut the lining to the shaped edge, slashing if necessary and finish in the same way (fig 108).

9 Pin heading tape to the top edge of the wrong side of the pelmet, turning in 13mm (½in) at each side edge. Use buttonhole thread to backstitch the ends and along the lower edge of the tape, stitching through to the buckram but not to the face fabric. Make pockets every 9-10cm

(3½-4in), backstitching from top to bottom of the tape (fig 108).

10 Fix the pelmet to the board with drawing pins as in fig 109, or stitch touch-and-close tape the back of the pelmet. Glue the matching strip to the front of the board.

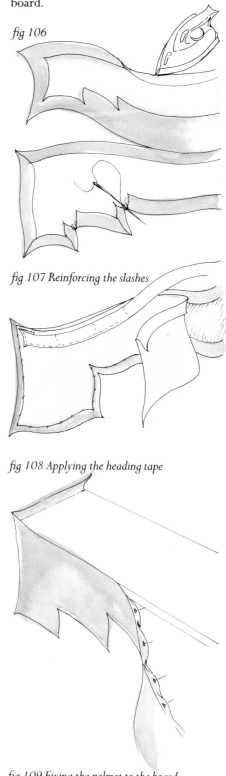

fig 106

fig 107 Reinforcing the slashes

fig 108 Applying the heading tape

fig 109 Fixing the pelmet to the board

LINED CURTAINS
WITH HEADING TAPE

For full instructions see page 21.

OTTOMAN COVER

Ottomans can be turned into seating units with a foam block cut to size on top and a simple loose cover. Choose firm, closely woven fabrics that are both crease-resistant and washable. Always make a welt for this type of cover, to hold it in position. Follow the same rules as for making loose covers (pages 15-16).

For a gathered frill allow one and a half to one and three quarter times the measurement round the ottoman. For equally spaced pleats, allow twice the measurement round the ottoman, and for a 50mm (2in) inverted pleat at each corner allow 20·5cm (8in) for each pleat.

YOU WILL NEED

*Fabric for cover and bias strips
Matching thread
Piping cord No 3
(boiled for 5 minutes and dried before use to
ensure it will not shrink when cleaned)
Zipper foot attachment for machine
Foam block cut to the size of the top*

To make

1 Make a cutting plan as in fig 110 to estimate the amount of fabric needed. Cut the top section and the welts, allowing 13mm (½in) turnings all round.

2 Prepare and cut enough bias strips and piping cord to fit round the ottoman twice (the top and bottom of the welt). Use the quick method on pages 109-10 (Sewing Guide).

3 Join the welts at each corner with a 13mm (½in) flat seam, making a continuous strip (fig 111). Seams on the corners give the cover extra strength as well as ensuring a good fit. Match and pin the seams of the welt to the corners of the top section.

4 Apply the piping and bias strip to the raw edge of the top section, snipping corners and joining the bias strips as in fig 32, page 29.

5 Apply bias strip and piping along the lower edge of the welt in the same way and machine stitch into position (fig 112).

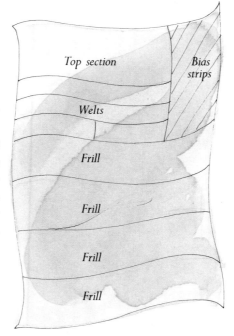

fig 110 Cutting plan for ottoman cover

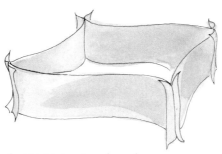

fig 111 Joining the welts at the corners

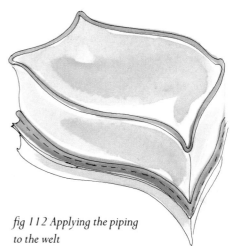

*fig 112 Applying the piping
to the welt*

6 Cut four pieces of fabric for the frill and join as for the welt sections, with the joins at each corner. Match pattern repeats carefully. Turn up a 13mm (½in) double hem at the lower edge and machine stitch into position. Make a 50mm (2in) inverted pleat at each side of the four seams and pin these to the seams at each corner (fig 113).

7 Pleat the rest of the fabric evenly between the corners so that the fabric fits into the length and width of the top section. Pin and tack into position. Machine stitch the frill to the welt using a zipper foot attachment to ensure that the stitching lies close to the piping cord.

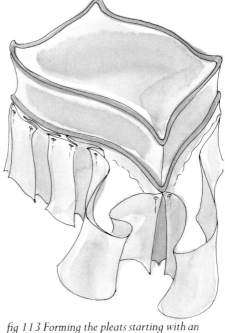

*fig 113 Forming the pleats starting with an
inverted pleat at each corner*

Colourfully to Bed

LOOSE HEADBOARD COVER WITH PIPING

TIFFANY LAMPSHADE

CURTAINS WITH TAB HEADINGS

BOX-PLEATED VALANCE

PLAIN PILLOWCASE

DUVET COVER WITH APPLIQUÉ DECORATION

You can let your imagination run riot in children's bedrooms with all kinds of bright and colourful effects you wouldn't dare use anywhere else in the house. It is important for young minds to be surrounded by easily definable shapes and colours to stimulate the imagination, making their room the ideal opportunity to enjoy yourself with primary colours, stencils and appliquéd shapes.

This bright, happy room has been painted sunny yellow and furnished in red, yellow and blue with fresh, easy-care fabrics, essential for a child's room. Plain royal blue curtains are thick enough to screen off light evenings and early morning sunshine, hung from a red painted curtain pole with simple tab headings. A duvet is warm and light and makes bed-making easy; here it is covered in a bright red fabric relieved by an appliquéd balloon motif — green, yellow and blue material applied in simple shapes. Appliqué is an excellent and effective way of using up left-over scraps of material from other features.

Red has also been chosen for the loose headboard cover, smartly piped for a neat finish, and the Tiffany lampshade hung well out of reach of curious fingers. To match the walls and a handy folding chair, pillowcase and bed valance are made in plain canary yellow fabric. Storage is essential for toys, books and clothes; here sturdy open shelving means that toys are visible as well as accessible, while a large wooden chest has been hand-painted and stencilled in matching primary colours.

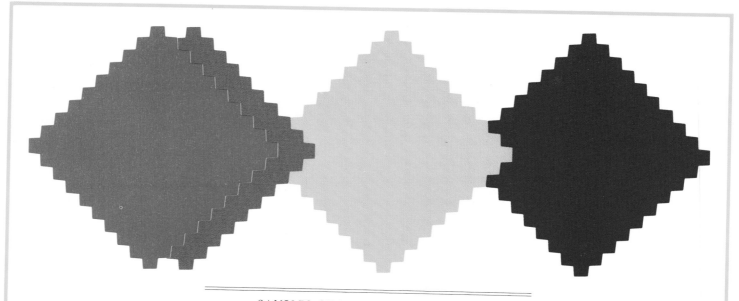

SAMPLES OF THE MATERIALS USED

1 Duvet and headboard cover
Cheerful pillar-box red washable 100% cotton sheeting.

2 Appliquéd balloon motif
Washable, bright green cotton poplin.

3 Pillow-case, valance and appliquéd balloon motif
Washable canary yellow cotton poplin.

4 Curtains and appliquéd balloon motif
Washable royal blue 100% cotton sheeting.

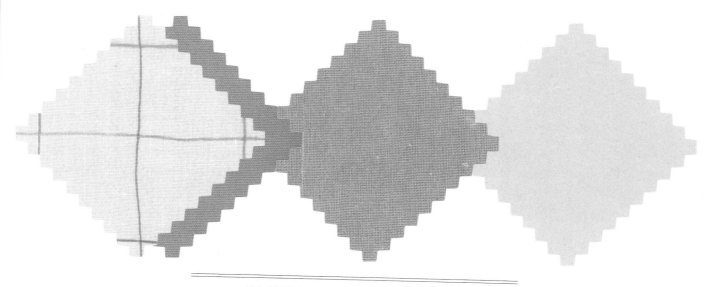

AN ALTERNATIVE COLOUR SCHEME

Children love bright primary colours but while they are still small you may prefer to tone them down into pinks and powder blues. A special room for a young toddler could not fail to please yet still be practical with this washable, pale pink sheeting in 100% cotton which features a cheerful grid design with contrasting deep pink, green and yellow lines. Use it to make a good-looking duvet cover, curtains and pillow-cases then pick out the fuchsia pink of the grid lines in a plain material to make matching piping for the duvet and headboard covers. Paint the walls pink too with easy-to-clean, pale pink, silk-finish emul-sion, while to create a gentle contrast, the main body of the headboard cover can be made in a powder blue washable cotton fabric and matched to a bed valance in the same material. For extra comfort use the plain pink, powder blue and multi-coloured grid fabrics to make an assortment of cushions, each appliquéd in a contrasting material with a different letter of the alphabet – one for each letter of the child's name, if it is not too long! The overall effect will be fresh and appealing yet practical: the perfect environment for both boys and girls with its clever pink and blue colour scheme.

Covering an existing headboard with a simple loose cover will give it a new lease of life. In this way you can renovate plain wooden headboards as well as plastic upholstered ones very effectively. Use fabric that matches or co-ordinates with bedcovers and curtains. Ready-quilted washable fabric gives excellent results. Alternatively, use sheeting, now available in a wide range of plain colours and patterns and quilt or pad the fabric yourself, following the instructions at the end of this section.

YOU WILL NEED

Quilted fabric or sheeting for front cover section
Matching fabric for back section
Matching thread
Piping cord No 3
(boiled for 5 minutes and dried before use to ensure it will not shrink when cleaned)
1·5m (1 ¾yds) strong cotton tape
Paper for making a pattern
Zipper foot attachment for machine

To make

1 Make a paper pattern of the headboard. Cut out a piece of fabric for the front section the size of the paper pattern plus 13mm (½in) turnings all round. For the back section use sheeting or unquilted matching fabric. If sheeting or quilted fabric is used for both sections, however,

the cover will be reversible. When the headboard is more than 38mm (1½in) thick it is advisable to insert a gusset between the front and back sections.

2 For a loose cover with a gusset, cut out and prepare enough piping cord and bias strip to fit round the top and side edges of both the back and front sections. Pin and tack as on page 29 (*Floor cushion*), clipping curves where necessary. Neaten the ends of the bias strip by pulling out the piping cord half an inch and turning in the ends as in fig 114.

3 Pin and tack the gusset to the front and back sections with right sides facing (fig 115) and machine stitch into position using a zipper foot attachment. Clip curves, trim seams and neaten edges.

4 Fold a 13mm (½in) double hem all round the lower edge of the cover and tack and machine stitch into position.

5 Sew six 23cm (9in) lengths of tape to the lower hems as in fig 116. Slip the cover on to the headboard and tie the tapes underneath to hold the cover firmly in place.

fig 114 To neaten the end of a bias strip, pull out the piping cord, trim and turn in the ends of the fabric

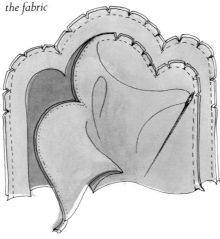

fig 115 Tacking the gusset in position

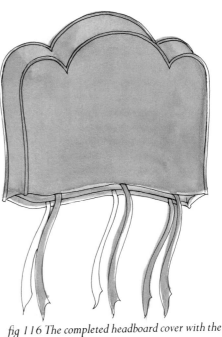

fig 116 The completed headboard cover with the six ties sewn into position

QUILTING METHOD

Although quilted fabric is available in a wide range of patterns and colours, you can choose any suitable fabric, such as cotton sheeting, and quilt it yourself. A layer of synthetic wadding is sandwiched between two pieces of co-ordinating fabrics, giving extra thickness, warmth and textural interest (see fig 66 on page 44).

Work rows of machine stitching 50-75mm (2-3in) apart, marking out lines from the centre of the fabric using tailor's chalk or long tacking stitches (see fig 66 on page 44). Quilt the fabric on the machine using a long straight stitch. If available, use a quilting gauge to ensure equal distances between the lines of stitching. Trim the raw edges and tack round the outside edge of the bedspread 25mm (1in) from the edge.

Except where the edge of the fabric will be concealed from view, raw edges should be neatly finished off. Cut a strip of bias binding 75mm (3in) wide from matching or contrasting fabric and apply this to the edge of the fabric on the right side. Tack and machine into position. Fold over to the wrong side, turning in 13mm (½in) and tack and slipstitch along the machine stitch line (fig 67).

TIFFANY LAMPSHADE

Tiffany lampshades spread the light well because of their shape and are well suited to both modern and informal interiors.

Many different fabrics can be used, including silks, cottons, polyester/cotton sheeting and broderie Anglaise. Choose crêpe-backed satin or a fine cotton lawn for the lining. This is stitched onto the frame in four sections before the cover fabric is applied. (Balloon linings are unsuitable for this shape of frame.)

To estimate the fabric needed, make a paper pattern of one quarter of the frame and add an allowance of 75mm (3in) all round. Four pieces of fabric this size cut on the cross grain will be required for the cover, and four pieces for the lining. Allow more when centring patterns. As a guide 0·75m (¾yd) fabric 90cm (36in) wide of both cover and lining fabric is usually sufficient for a Tiffany frame 25·5-30·5cm (10-12in) across the base.

YOU WILL NEED

Tiffany style lampshade frame (fig 158)
Lampshade tape
0·75m (¾yd) fabric 90cm (36in) wide for the outer cover
0·75m (¾yd) fabric 90cm (36in) wide for the lining
Good quality steel dressmaking pins or glass-headed pins
Matching thread
Trimming
Clear-drying adhesive

To make

1 For a plastic-coated frame it is only necessary to tape the four struts on to which the fabric will be stitched, as well as the top and bottom rings. Otherwise, tape the whole frame (see fig 24 on page 25).

2 Place the lining fabric on to one quarter of the frame with the wrong side outside. Pin in position, starting each corner as in fig 117. Ease out the fullness and adjust the pins until the fabric is smooth and taut over the frame.

3 Working from right to left, oversew the fabric to the frame using lengths of matching thread. Start at the top and work round the four sides of the section. Trim off the surplus fabric close to the stitching at both side edges (fig 118) and work the other three quarters of the frame in the same way, pinning and sewing over the previous line of stitching.

4 Pin and stitch the four sections of the cover fabric over the lining as before, but with the right sides outside, using the same struts for stitching. Trim off the surplus fabric at the top and bottom rings close to the stitching.

5 Fold over the lining to the front of the lampshade at the top and bottom rings and stitch neatly with one long stitch and one short one alternately (fig 119). Cut off surplus fabric close to the stitching.

6 Neaten the four side struts by covering them with a bias strip of matching fabric. Cut four strips the length of the struts by 32mm (1¼in) wide. Turn in and press the edges to make a strip 13mm (½in) wide. Secure these to the struts using a small knife to spread the adhesive on to the wrong side of the strips. Stretch the strip gently as it is applied to the strut to obtain a neat finish (fig 120).

7 Stitch a lampshade trimming to the top and bottom of the lampshade (see figs 214 to 215, *Classic lampshade with balloon lining*, page 106, or make a frill to decorate the lower edge.

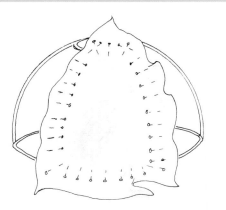

fig 117 Pinning the lining to the frame

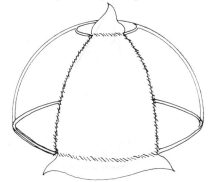

fig 118 Oversewing the lining into place

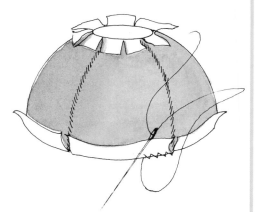

fig 119 Stitching the lining to the frame

fig 120 Neatening the struts with bias

CURTAINS WITH TAB HEADINGS

These headings can be used for café curtains as well as for lined or unlined curtains that are hung from a pole. Loops or tabs are made separately and sewn to the head of the curtains, using matching or contrasting fabric. Tab headings are an ideal way of emphasizing a decorative pole, but alternatively, you could easily paint a plain pole in a matching or contrasting colour for an attractive over-all effect.

If you use these headings for your curtains you will find you can economize on the amount of fabric required. To estimate the amount of fabric needed for the curtain width, use approximately one and a half times the measurement of the pole.

YOU WILL NEED

Curtain fabric
Matching thread
Lining sateen (optional)
Extra fabric for tabs (see below)

To make

1 Make up the curtains as for a lined curtain (page 21), turning in the face fabric 50mm (2in) at the top edge of the curtain, or as for an unlined curtain (page 81) making a 25mm (1in) double machined hem at the top edge. Omit heading tapes.

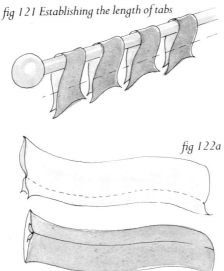

fig 121 Establishing the length of tabs

fig 122a

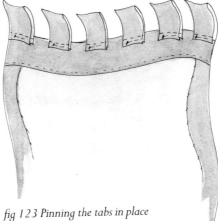

fig 122b Stitching the tabs

fig 123 Pinning the tabs in place

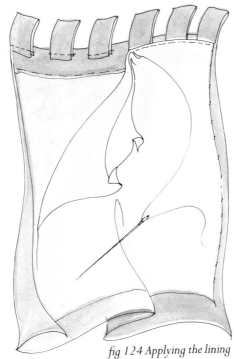

fig 124 Applying the lining

2 Measure the top of the curtain to decide how many taps are needed and mark their positions. Allow approximately 10-12·5cm (4-5in) between each tab and make the finished width of the tab 25-64mm (1-2½in) depending on the fabric and the effect required. The length of the tab is determined by placing a piece of fabric or string round the pole to assess the measurement needed. The curtain should normally hang 38-64mm (1½-2½in) below the pole. To this measurement add 50mm (2in) for turnings (fig 121).

3 For a tab measuring 30·5 × 5cm (12 × 2in) (finished measurement), cut a piece of fabric on the straight grain 35·5 × 12·5cm (14in × 5in). Fold in half lengthwise with right sides together, taking 13mm (½in) turnings. Tack and machine stitch (fig 122a).

4 Trim the seam to 6mm (¼in) and turn to the right side. Press the seam so that it is positioned in the centre of the tab (fig 122b), turning in the raw edges 13mm (½in) at each end of the tab. Press and slipstitch.

5 For an unlined curtain pin the tabs to the top of the wrong side of the curtain with the seam inside, having one tab at each side edge of the curtain and arranging the others so that they have equal spaces between them (fig 123). Tack and machine stitch each tab in position 6mm (¼in) from the top edge.

6 For a lined curtain insert the tabs between the lining and the face fabric, positioning them as for the unlined curtain. Tack the tabs to the wrong side of the face fabric. Place the lining over the tabs and tack in position. Work two rows of machine stitching on the right side of the curtain 6mm (¼in) from the top edge (fig 124).

BOX-PLEATED VALANCE

For full instructions see pages 46 and 57.

DUVET COVER WITH APPLIQUÉ DECORATION

Duvet covers are best made from easily washable fabric such as polyester/cotton sheeting. Use wide width fabrics to avoid too many seams.

An appliqué or other form of surface decoration will brighten plain duvet covers so long as they are able to withstand frequent washing. Keep decorations simple and strong, choosing bold shapes and colours rather than intricate embroidery that is time-consuming to work and which will not withstand hard wear. Alternatively, make the covers reversible by mixing co-ordinating fabrics, using a large print on one side and small one on the other.

Make the duvet cover a little larger than the duvet itself so that the filling is not constricted when the duvet is in use. Measure carefully to estimate for fabric requirements. Work French seams where possible as these enclose all raw edges and make the cover more hardwearing. Openings can be finished with touch-and-close fastener, press studs or a zip fastener.

Remember to work your appliquéd motifs before the cover is made up.

YOU WILL NEED

Single size duvet cover:
(approx. 3m (3 ½yds) fabric 228cm (90in) wide)
Double size duvet cover:
(approx. 4·5m (5yd) fabric 228cm (90in) wide
Fabric for appliqué (optional)
Non-woven interfacing
Matching thread

To make

1 Measure the width and the length of the duvet and cut out two pieces of fabric to these measurements plus 13mm (½in) turnings all round.

2 Appliqué the motif as detailed below.

3 Pin and tack the two sections with wrong sides together to make French

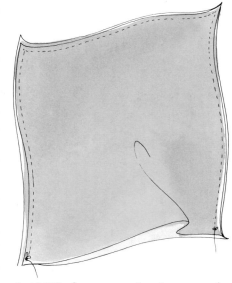

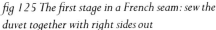

fig 125 The first stage in a French seam: sew the duvet together with right sides out

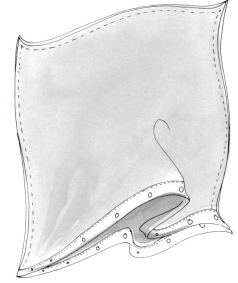

fig 126 The duvet is turned inside out and the three sides tacked and sewn to complete the French seams. Press studs, touch-and-close or zip fastenings are then applied

seams. Machine round three sides leaving the lower short end unstitched (fig 125). Trim seams to 3mm (⅛in). Turn the wrong sides outside and press the seams. Finish the French seams by tacking and machining round the three sides (fig 126).

4 Make a 13mm (½in) double hem at the opening edge of the duvet cover and sew on press studs every 10cm (4in) along this edge (fig 126). Alternatively, sew on touch-and-close fastener or insert a zip fastener.

Appliqué motif
Use initials, numbers, or any bold simple shape for a child's duvet cover. Several suggestions are illustrated opposite. Draw out the design first on a sheet of paper or card.

1 Trace the design on to a piece of non-woven interfacing and pin and tack this to the back of the front section of the duvet cover (fig 127). Reverse the shape if necessary.

2 Cut a piece of the appliqué fabric slightly larger than the design. Tack this to the right side of the duvet cover, matching grain lines and taking care that it corresponds with the interfacing material on the wrong side (fig 128).

3 On the wrong side of the cover sew along the traced lines on the interfacing material with a small zigzag stitch (fig 129).

4 Turn cover to the right side and cut away the surplus appliqué fabric close up to the stitching, using a sharp pair of scissors (fig 130).

5 Work another row of close zigzag or satin stitch round the motif on the right side covering the first run of stitching (fig 130).

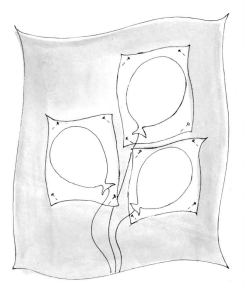

fig 127 Pin the backing fabric to the wrong side

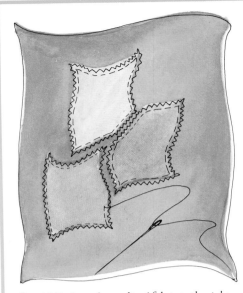

fig 128 Tacking the appliqué fabric to the right side

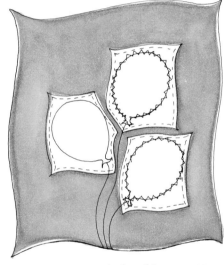

fig 129 Stitching the backing fabric in position

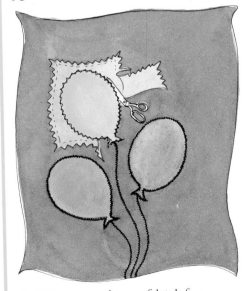

fig 130 Trimming the spare fabric before completing the close zigzag stitching

Country Cottage Charm

CAFÉ CURTAINS

QUILTED PLACE MATS

SQUAB CUSHION WITH TIES

DRESS CURTAINS WITH FRILLED
TIE-BACKS

Even a tiny town kitchen can capture the atmosphere of a country
cottage with careful choice of furniture and fabrics. Here the traditional
pine dresser and sturdy kitchen table have been scaled down from the
original designs to fit today's more modestly sized rooms and set the mood
for pretty country floral prints, copper pans and fine
china kept on display.

The deep pink and green rambling briar rose design on a cream
background which has been chosen for curtains and cushions is strong
and fresh, echoed by the rosebud motif on the predominantly white
china. An uninspiring view over the sink has been screened by a smart
café curtain, hung on a narrow brass rail with tab headings and the
window framed by a pair of dress curtains, purely for decoration and kept
out of the way with attractive ruffled tie-backs using the same material.
Squab cushions made from latex or foam pads are ideal for adding
comfort to usually hard wooden kitchen chairs and these have been
covered in matching flower print fabric with ties to stop them slipping
off; a large square cushion to match also softens a wooden rocking chair.

To complete the co-ordinated effect, the fabric has
even been used to make a set of quilted place mats, edged in deep green to
match the trim on the squab cushions. It is this combination of warm pine
furniture and fresh country florals that is guaranteed to conjure up the
cottage atmosphere of home baking and home-made preserves.

SAMPLES OF THE MATERIALS USED

1 Curtains, tie-backs, large square cushion and squab cushions
Red, green and cream 100% cotton print with a rambling briar rose and bird pattern.

2 Piping on tie-backs, squab cushions and place mats
Dark green bias binding picks out the darkest tone of the print.

3 Place mats
Ready-quilted red, green and cream cotton in the same design as the fabric used for the curtains and cushions.

4 Wallcovering
Cream, silk-finish, easily cleaned emulsion paint for a plain background.

AN ALTERNATIVE COLOUR SCHEME

Old-fashioned country style fabrics look particularly good teamed with mellow pine units and this fresh cotton print in earthy colours is the ideal alternative for small kitchens where a larger pattern may look too busy. In 100% cotton with a tiny terracotta, cream and brown design, the main fabric will easily conjure up a country farmhouse atmosphere when used to make pretty kitchen curtains with matching tie-backs, or square and squab cushions for the traditional wooden chairs. These can all be finished with piping or trimming in a washable, plain beige cotton fabric to complement the background of browns and creams, while the terracotta of the design makes a good contrast picked out in a plain, washable fabric and made up into quilted place-mats with the same beige fabric trim. Whatever their size, busy printed fabrics like these country cotton prints need a relatively plain background if they are not to get lost and confused among the everyday kitchen paraphernalia, and an easy-to-clean, silk-finish emulsion paint in cream on the walls not only continues the cream background of the curtains and cushions, but provides a pleasant relaxing environment to work in too.

CAFÉ CURTAINS

Café curtains are usually hung on poles or rods half way up a window to screen an unpleasant view or to give privacy. Unlined curtains allow more light to filter through than lined ones.

Allow one and a half times the pole measurement for an unlined scalloped heading. Pleated headings need more fullness (fig 131). Face the heading for a neat finish. If a stiffer heading is required, insert a strip of bonded interfacing between the curtain fabric and the facing.

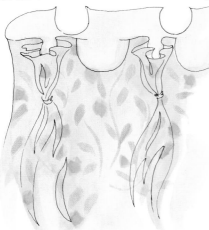

fig 131 Scalloped heading with pleats

UNLINED CAFÉ CURTAIN WITH SCALLOPED HEADING

YOU WILL NEED

Curtain fabric
Matching thread
Heading tape
Paper for pattern
Plate or compass to trace shapes
Tailor's chalk

To make

1 Make up the curtain as for an unlined curtain (page 81), allowing sufficient fabric at the top of the curtain to make the heading, that is the depth of the scallops plus 75mm (3in) for the hem.

2 Make a paper pattern, cutting it to the width of the curtain and approximately 30·5cm (12in) deep.

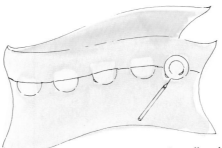

fig 132 Marking out the scalloped edge along the pencil guideline

3 Draw a line 75mm (3in) from the top and mark out the scalloped edge as in fig 132 starting at the folded edge in the centre. Work out the size of the scallops to fit into the space available, making the diameter of each scallop 10-15cm (4-6in) and leaving approximately 38mm (1½in) between each one.

4 Use a plate or a compass to draw the shapes then cut round them carefully. (For pleated scallops allow more space between each scallop for the pleat to be formed – see *Curtains with hand-made triple-pleated heading* on page 103.)

fig 133 Stitching the scallops, and clipping the curves

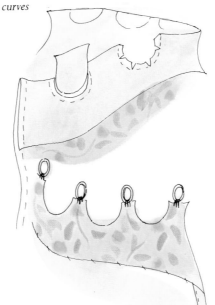

fig 134 Finishing the facing and attaching the rings

5 On the right side of the curtain fold over the top edge of the curtain the depth of the scallop plus 75mm (3in) for a hem allowance.

6 Place the pattern to the folded edge at the top and mark round the scallops with a sharp piece of tailor's chalk. Tack and machine stitch on this line.

7 Clip curves and corners and cut out scallops 6mm (¼in) from the line of stitching (fig 133).

8 Turn the facing to the wrong side of the curtain and press. Finish with a 13mm (½in) double hem at the lower edge. Attach rings to each scallop (fig 134).

LINED CAFÉ CURTAINS WITH TAB HEADINGS

Tab headings look very attractive on café curtains, and can also be used for lined and unlined curtains that are hung from a pole. Loops are applied to the head of the curtains using matching, co-ordinating or contrasting fabric. Wide furnishing braid is an effective substitute.

QUILTED PLACE MATS

For full instructions see page 76

SQUAB CUSHION WITH TIES

These cushions are ideal for dining room and kitchen chairs, where they can be matched to other furnishings. You can use an identical fabric for curtains, table-cloth, napkins, place mats, and so on, or one that co-ordinates well. Choose hard wearing fabrics such as furnishing cotton, linen union or repp (corded cloth). Alternatively, use corduroy, velvet or other upholstery fabrics, but remember these need to be dry cleaned and cannot be washed.

Use latex or plastic foam sheets 13-19mm (½-¾in) thick for the pad. Either buy a suitably shaped pad from a soft furnishing department or make one yourself, cutting out the foam to the shape required. Thin sheets of foam can be cut with a pair of scissors, but a sharp knife is necessary when cutting thicker pieces. Cover the pad with calico or other cotton fabric to protect it from wear.

YOU WILL NEED

*1m (1¼yd) fabric 120cm (48in) wide
(for an average-size chair seat)
Matching thread
Piping cord No 3
(boiled for 5 minutes and dried before use to
ensure it will not shrink when cleaned)
Zipper foot attachment for machine
Paper for making pattern*

To make

1 Make a pattern of the chair seat by placing a sheet of paper on the seat and drawing all round. Fold in half lengthwise to check that both sides are equal. Make any adjustments necessary, making sure that the pattern fits well at the back of the chair. Mark the positions for the ties (fig 135).

2 Using the paper pattern cut out the foam shape, marking it with a felt-tip pen. Cover the pad with calico or other cotton fabric to protect it from wear and tear.

3 Cut out the top and bottom sections of the cushion cover, using the paper pattern and allowing 13mm (½in) turnings all round. Mark the positions for the ties at the back of the top section with tailor's chalk or tailor's tacks.

4 Cut and prepare enough bias strips and piping cord to measure round the outer edge of the cushion (use the quick method on page 109, Sewing Guide). Pin and tack this to the raw edge of the top section of the cover as in fig 136. Machine stitch into position using a zipper foot attachment. Mark the position for the opening at the back of the cushion cover (fig 136). Allow approximately 25·5-28cm (10-11in) so that the cover can be removed easily.

5 Make the ties by cutting two strips of fabric on the straight grain 32mm (1¼in) wide by 61cm (24in) long. Fold the strips in half lengthwise and press. Turn in edges 6mm (¼in) and press and machine stitch into position (fig 137). Fold each strip in half and apply to the right side of the top section in the positions marked.

6 With the right sides together pin and tack the bottom section to the top section. Machine stitch all round the cushion cover leaving the opening unstitched. Neaten the seams and clip curves where necessary.

7 Turn the cover to the right side and insert the pad. Close the opening with slipstitch for a neat finish.

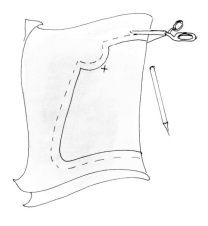

fig 135 Making the pattern – the unbroken line is for cutting the foam pad; the dotted line is for the fabric

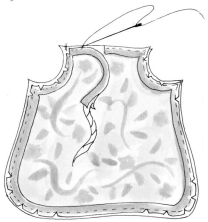

fig 136 Tacking the bias strip and piping cord to the top section of the cushion cover and clipping curves for ease of fit

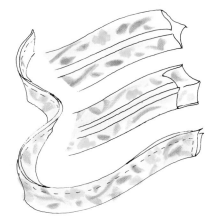

fig 137 Making the ties for the back of the cushion: each strip is folded in half then the edges are pressed in and stitched into place

DRESS CURTAINS WITH FRILLED TIE-BACKS

Dress curtains are used purely as a decorative feature to soften a window or where there is little space at either side of the window frame. The backs can be plain, frilled as in the photograph, or ruffled. They can be combined with blinds to frame the window, or treated as decoration only where flowing fabric could be a hazard. Fix them on to small tracks in the position required.

Dress curtains are constructed in the same way as lined or unlined curtains, but when estimating their width measure only the space they will take up, not the window size. Allow approximately twice this measurement.

RUFFLED TIE-BACK

YOU WILL NEED

Fabric
Matching thread
Curtain gathering tape
Rings for slipping over a hook in the wall

To make

1 For a 12·5cm (5in) wide ruffled tie-back estimate its length by tying a piece of string or fabric round the curtains and cut a strip of fabric twice this length by 25·5cm (10in) in width.

2 With right sides together fold the fabric in half lengthwise and pin and tack the two short edges together as in fig 138. Machine stitch in place and turn the fabric to the right side. Press.

3 Apply a simple curtain gathering tape to the wrong side of the tie-back, positioning it over the raw edges (fig 139). Buttonhole-stitch a ring to each end and pull up the cords to the length required (fig 139). Tie them up neatly to finish.

PIPED AND FRILLED TIE-BACK

YOU WILL NEED

Fabric
Matching thread
Piping cord No 3
(boiled for 5 minutes and dried before use to ensure it will not shrink when cleaned)

To make

1 Estimate the length of fabric for the tie-back as above and cut two pieces plus 6mm (¼in) all round for turnings. For the frill cut two pieces at least one and a half times the length of the tie-back and twice the required frill width, plus 13mm (½in). Prepare sufficient piping cord using the quick method on page 109 (see Sewing Guide).

2 Fold the fabric for the frill in half to eliminate any hems and run two rows of gathering thread 6mm (¼in) and 13mm (½in) from the raw edges. Pull up the threads and arrange the gathers so the frill is the same length as the tie-back. Machine.

3 Turn under 6mm (¼in) all round on the tie-back and slipstitch the frill and piping to the long sides as in fig 140. Turn under the short ends and buttonhole stitch rings to each end (fig 141).

4 Turn under 6mm (¼in) on the second piece of fabric. Slipstitch it to the back of the tie-back to cover all raw edges.

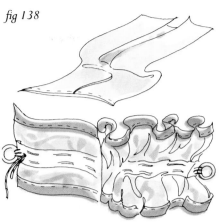

fig 138

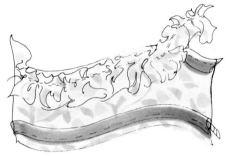

fig 139 Forming the ruffled tie-back. After the gathering tape has been applied, rings are sewn to each end

fig 140 Tacking the frill to the front section

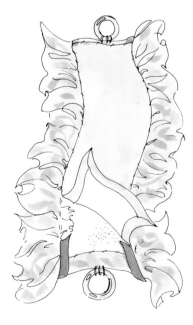

fig 141 Slipstitching the lining to the back of the tie-back to enclose all the raw edges

A Place in the Sun

ROLLER BLIND

QUILTED PLACE MATS

QUILTED OVEN MITT

TEA COSY

You can create your own sunshine corner anywhere in the house with clever use of sunny yellow fabric and accessories. This kitchen lacked life and character of its own, fitted with attractive but plain white cupboards and units trimmed in grey and a large picture window which let in plenty of light but was somewhat featureless.

Roller blinds are quick and easy to make and are ideal for kitchen windows where they can be simply pulled up and down without fuss; in a brilliant, plain yellow fabric they can transform the room with a sunny glow whatever the weather. Here they have been matched to a wide range of bright accessories: yellow checkered storage containers, mugs, tea-towels, harlequin-coloured crockery, even a canary-coloured coffee maker. The same yellow fabric as the blind has been quilted lengthways and made up into oven gloves, place mats and egg cosies which are practical as well as pretty.

Neutral rooms such as these can be highlighted any way you please and make quite a good basis for starting a scheme; yellow is a fine cheery colour to come down to in the morning but there is no reason why you shouldn't choose red, blue, pink or your favourite shade as your accent colour. Kitchen appliances and accessories are available in a wide choice of colours these days and it is easy to buy a few metres of matching fabric to make up into a whole range of useful items for a fully co-ordinated look.

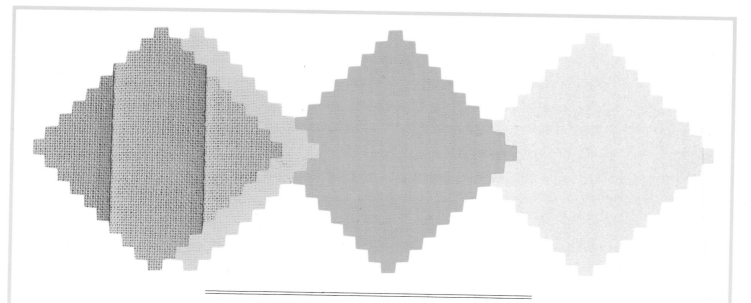

SAMPLES OF THE MATERIALS USED

1 Oven glove, place mat and egg cosy
Brilliant yellow 100% cotton quilted lengthways. The same fabric is used unquilted for the blind.

2 Binding for oven glove, place mat and egg cosy
Pale yellow glazed 100% cotton tone with the main fabric.

3 Blind
For a truly co-ordinated look, the brilliant yellow cotton fabric is stiffened for use as a blind.

4 Wallcovering
Pale blue-grey easy-to-clean, silk finish emulsion paint.

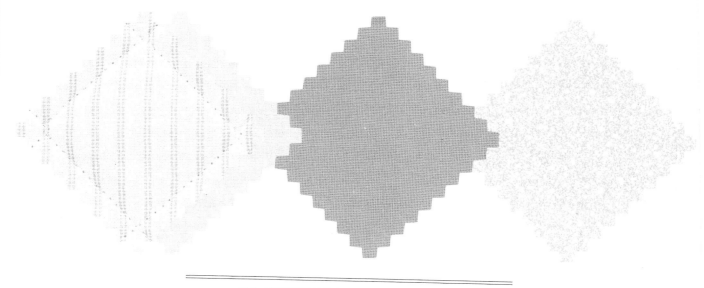

AN ALTERNATIVE COLOUR SCHEME

Change the accent colour in the kitchen from sunny yellow to pretty pink to make a gentler start to the day while imparting a fresh summery feel all year round; teamed with clean white and soft sky blue the atmosphere is cool and relaxing while the blending of colours is unusually refreshing. A roller blind in pure pink cotton sheds a rosy glow on the greyest winter morning, while pink and white candy striped fabric in 100% quilted cotton for the oven glove, place mat and egg cosy looks perennially fresh, especially when trimmed or piped in crisp white cotton. If you decide to use pastel shades in a hardwork-ing area such as the kitchen, it is essential to choose materials that are easy to clean. However pretty you make it, this is one room that must work efficiently. This blue vinyl wallpaper can be wiped down as often as necessary to mop up spills and splashes and prevent an accumulation of kitchen grime. Pure cotton is another good choice because it can be washed time and again and still come up looking bright. There are several modern ranges of crockery and cutlery to match this scheme, which would also look good with pretty old-fashioned china for a more homely atmosphere.

ROLLER BLINDS

Roller blinds are a practical way of treating windows in kitchens and bathrooms. They roll up to the top of the window round a wooden or aluminium roller, allowing the maximum amount of light into the room. A strongly patterned fabric will make your window a prominent feature. Alternatively you could decorate it yourself with fabric paints and stencils.

Use specially stiffened blind fabrics which are available in wide widths to avoid joins. Alternatively, stiffen the fabric yourself using a special spray-on or liquid stiffener. Choose smooth, closely woven fabrics for this, such as furnishing cottons or linens, as these give the best results. Test a small piece of the fabric first to assess how much stiffening is needed. As the fabric may shrink, stiffen before cutting to the size required. It will not be necessary to make hems as the fabric should not fray after it has been stiffened.

Roller blinds are quick and easy to make using the special kits available. These consist of a roller with a spring and a metal cap at one end, and a metal cap with a pin to fix on to the other end once the roller has been cut to the size required. Two brackets are also provided to fix the blind in position at the side or in front of the window. (Full manufacturer's instructions should be provided for fixing them.) Also included in the kits is a pull-cord and a batten to give weight to the lower edge of the blind. These kits are extremely useful and do not limit you to a restricted choice of fabrics.

Make the blind from one width of fabric if possible as seams in the fabric make it more difficult for the blind to roll smoothly round the roller. On a wide window use more than one blind if necessary.

It is very important to make sure that the fabric is cut perfectly square. Otherwise, it will not roll round the roller correctly – and will not hang well either. Use a T-square or the edge of a square or rectangular table when cutting out.

YOU WILL NEED

Stiffened fabric
Matching thread
Roller blind kit
Trimming (optional)
Clear adhesive

To make

1 Decide where you wish to position the blind (inside or outside the window recess) and fix the two brackets in position. Measure carefully to find the necessary length for the roller and cut this to the size required.

2 Measure the length of the window and cut out the fabric to the exact width of the roller by the length of the window plus a 15cm (6in) allowance for turnings. This will ensure that there is enough fabric to make a casing at the lower edge of the roller blind and for a little of the fabric to roll round the roller at the top of the window.

3 Make a casing for the batten at the lower edge by turning up first 13mm (½in) and then 38mm (1½in). To make it easier to handle, first mark a guide line in pencil and secure the casing with a little adhesive. Machine with a zigzag stitch (fig 142).

4 Place the roller on the right side of the fabric as in fig 143, positioning it over the guide line marked on the roller. Apply a little adhesive to hold it in position while the tacks are knocked in.

5 Trim the wooden batten to the length required for the lower casing and insert as in fig 144. Thread the cord through the acorn fitting and screw to the wrong side of the blind.

6 The lower edge of the blind may be trimmed with a piece of decorative braid or fringe (fig 145). Alternatively, cut a piece of fabric to the shape required, following the instructions for making pelmets on page 56, and fix it to the back of the casing with adhesive.

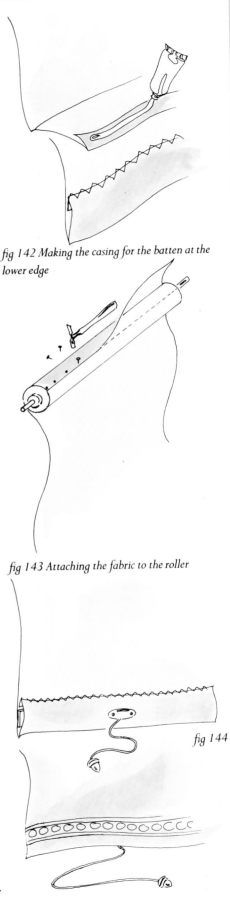

fig 142 *Making the casing for the batten at the lower edge*

fig 143 *Attaching the fabric to the roller*

fig 144

fig 145 *Finishing off the lower edge*

QUILTED ACCESSORIES

Ready quilted fabric is available in many designs, often co-ordinating with an existing furnishing range, but you can quilt fabric yourself. While it is particularly suitable for articles which require some sort of insulation, it works just as well on small matching accessories such as oven gloves, egg cosies, pot-holders and appliance covers for the kitchen; pretty toilet bags, make-up bags, tissue-box covers and covered hangers for the bedroom and bathroom. All quick and simple to make, they add a special finishing touch to a thoughtfully furnished room.

PLACE MATS

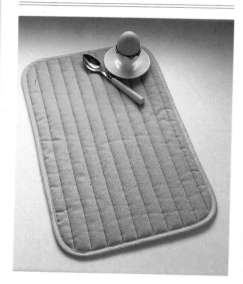

Make place mats in simple shapes such as circles, oblongs, squares or rectangles, to a size that best suits your table. An average size for a circular mat is about 25·5cm (10in) and for a rectangular one 40·5×30·5cm (16×12in) but these sizes can be varied to suit requirements. Lay a place setting on the table and measure the amount of space it takes up. Cut out sheets of paper to this size and experiment to see whether it works well on the individual table.

Use washable fabrics in 'linen look' acrylics, dress and furnishing cottons, seersuckers, or ginghams, choosing fabrics that do not stretch or fray easily.

Don't forget Easter and Christmas style prints for festive meals. Ready-quilted fabrics make excellent table mats, or you can quilt your own fabric and bind the raw edges.

To make a heat-resistant mat, sandwich a piece of latex rubber and cotton heat-resistant fabric between two pieces of material and bind the raw edges.

OBLONG QUILTED PLACE MATS

YOU WILL NEED

2 pieces of fabric 40·5×30·5cm (16×12in)
Thin sheet of synthetic wadding 40·5×30·5cm (16×12in)
Bias binding 38-50mm (1½-2in) wide or bias strips in matching or contrasting fabric

To make

1 Cut out the two pieces of fabric 40·5×30·5cm (16×12in) and trim the piece of thin synthetic wadding approximately 6mm (¼in) smaller all round.

2 Sandwich the wadding between the two pieces of fabric and tack them together from the centre outwards to hold the fabric firmly in position (fig 146).

3 Quilt the fabric on the machine as on page 44 or, if the fabric has a suitable pattern, machine along the predominating lines of the design (fig 147) making a random or regular design.

4 Make rounded corners using a plate as a guide and trim the edges of the mat.

5 Cut enough bias binding or bias strips 38-50mm (1½-2in) wide to measure round the outer edge of the mat (using the quick method on pages 109-10, Sewing Guide). Apply this to the right side of the mat, matching raw edges and taking 13mm (½in) turnings. Tack and machine stitch into position (fig 148).

6 Fold over the strip to the wrong side of the mat on to the line of machine stitching and slipstitch in place as in fig 149. Alternatively, topstitch on the right side.

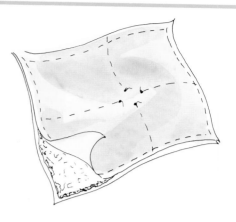

fig 146 *Tacking the wadding between the two layers of fabric*

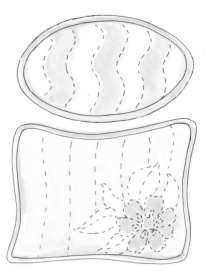

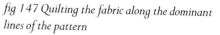

fig 147 *Quilting the fabric along the dominant lines of the pattern*

fig 148

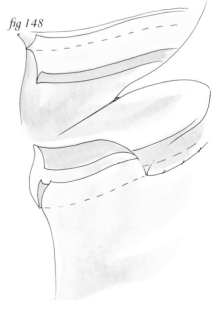

fig 149 *Applying the bias binding to enclose the raw edges*

QUILTED OVEN MITT

YOU WILL NEED

Quilted fabric
Matching thread
Bias binding 38×50mm (1 ½×2in) wide or
bias strips in a matching or contrasting colour
Paper for pattern

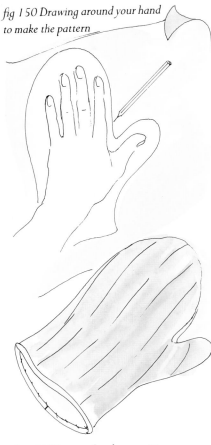

fig 150 Drawing around your hand
to make the pattern

fig 151 The completed oven mitt

To make

1 Make a pattern for the mitt by placing your hand flat on the paper with thumb outstretched and drawing round it allowing 25mm (1in) all round (fig 150). The finished glove should be fairly loose fitting and come at least 75mm (3in) up the wrist. Cut two pieces of fabric.

2 With right sides together, tack and machine stitch all round except the cuff and neaten the raw edges.

3. Turn to the right side and apply bias binding round the wrist, finishing in a small loop so that the glove can be hung on a hook near the cooker. Tack and machine stitch in position.

TEA COSY

YOU WILL NEED

Quilted fabric
Matching thread
Piping cord No 3
(boiled for 5 minutes and dried before use to
ensure it will not shrink when cleaned)
Paper for pattern

To make

1 Make a paper pattern in the traditional semi-circular shape to fit your teapot; average size is approximately 23cm (9in) high by 30·5cm (12in) across. Cut two pieces of quilted fabric adding 13mm (½in) all round and prepare sufficient piping to trim the seams and lower edge using the quick method on page 109 (Sewing Guide).

2 With right sides facing, stitch the piping and the two halves of the tea cosy together allowing 13mm (½in) seam allowance. Notch the seams.

3 Turn the tea cosy right sides out and press. Pin the piping round the lower edge of the cosy, matching the raw edges of the piping to the wrong side of the cosy, then slipstitch the piping neatly into place for a smart finish.

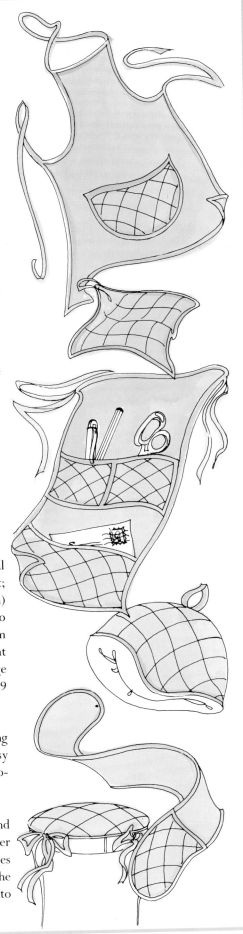

Pretty and Cool

UNLINED CURTAINS WITH FRILL

SHOWER CURTAINS

COVERED COAT HANGER

ROUND BOXED CUSHION WITH
ZIP OPENING

TOWEL TRIMS

*Co-ordinated fabric ranges make room planning a pleasure,
as this pretty bathroom demonstrates. Using a variety of fabric designs
based on peach and aquamarine, the blue has been chosen as main colour
for a cool, sophisticated effect, while the en-suite bedroom shown on
pages 40-1 has cleverly selected the same designs in the peach with a
touch of aquamarine.*

*Here the blue features strongly, picked out and painted
on walls and the side of a traditional Victorian claw-feet bath, while
sanitary-ware, furniture and tiles are kept a clean, plain white to
highlight the effect. Curtains made up in a tiny peach-sprigged fabric
are edged with a pretty frill to match the cushions on a white painted
Lloyd loom chair: a square frilled cushion and a tailored round welted
cushion seat to fit the chair are both made in the same sprig design but in
aquamarine finished with plain peach piping. A wide turquoise and white
striped fabric with a narrow peach stripe running through it from the
same range makes super shower curtains with a detachable plastic lining
to help protect from splashes.*

*Look out for those little touches which really give a room
that special classy finish: soaps and accessories in co-ordinating colours,
and matching towels which can be trimmed to suit your décor with strips
of contrasting or complementary fabric; or thread appropriately coloured
ribbons through bands of broderie anglaise.*

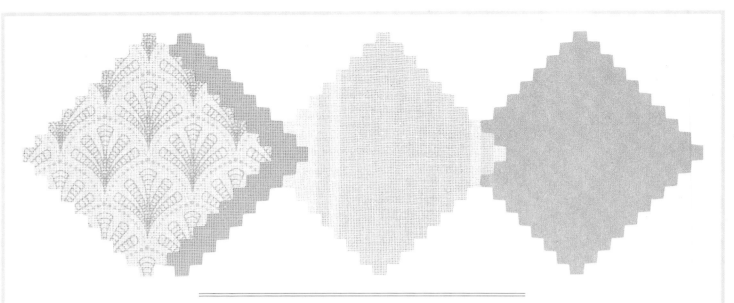

SAMPLES OF THE MATERIALS USED

1 Curtains, square frilled cushion and round cushions
Washable 100% cotton in a delicate aquamarine and peach sprig design.

2 Piping
Washable, plain 100% cotton in cool peach picks out the second colour of
the main prints.

3 Shower curtain
Aquamarine, peach and white Regency stripe in 100% washable cotton
with detachable waterproof nylon lining.

4 Wallcovering and side of bath
Easy-to-clean, silk-finish emulsion paint in matching aquamarine.

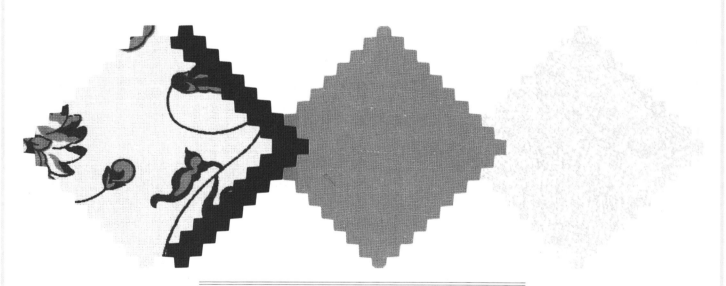

AN ALTERNATIVE COLOUR SCHEME

Simply use a different range of shades of blue and you can totally alter the mood of this pretty bathroom. Instead of warm peach and aquamarine, a bold royal blue combined with white has all the freshness of a Dutch tile. A crisp blue and white floral print in washable cotton could be the starting point for a light, cool scheme: use it to make curtains with both round and square cushion covers to match, picking up the deep blue of the design in plain blue cotton fabric for smart piping to accentuate their shape. The lighter china blue of the floral print could also be picked out and matched to a plain, washable cotton fabric, then used to make the shower curtain with a detachable waterproof lining. The deep colour and clarity of the blue and white design adds weight and interest to the room; it would be given most impact if the surrounding walls were kept fairly muted. This practical pale blue wallpaper would be ideal, the marbled effect creating an ice-cool background for the deeper blues and with the added advantage that it is washable. It is the clever mixing of different shades of blue that prevent such a colour scheme from being too glum or too chilly. Accent colours can easily be introduced if necessary, such as scarlet, lavender or jade.

UNLINED CURTAIN
WITH SINGLE FRILL

Lightweight unlined curtains have advantages in several situations. From a practical point of view, they are quick to launder, iron and replace, making them suitable for kitchens, as long as they are not used anywhere near a source of heat like the cooker or an electric toaster. Their light appearance fits them for summery rooms where the window is often open, minimizing the division between outdoors and in, while affording some privacy and moving gracefully in a gentle breeze. In a bathroom, where both good ventilation and privacy are important, they are ideal. Detachable linings can be added to this style of curtain if needed at times to provide extra insulation or to cut out more light.

YOU WILL NEED

Curtain fabric
Heading tape
Matching thread

To make

1 Measure up and estimate the amount of fabric needed as for lined curtains (page 21). Cut out the fabric, matching patterns and cutting off the selvedges and joining widths where necessary. Use a flat fell seam so that all raw edges are enclosed (page 108, Sewing Guide). For a curtain without a frill turn in the two side edges of the curtain and make a 13mm (½in) double hem. Turn up a 25mm (1in) double hem at the lower edge. Machine stitch in position.

2 For a frilled edge fold in the two side edges and the lower hem 13mm (½in) and press along the folds. Measure round the curtain to obtain the length needed to make the frill. Allow one and a half to twice this measurement.

3 For a 75mm (3in) wide frill cut strips of fabric 10cm (4in) by the length required, joining them if necessary with French seams to obtain the required length. Turn

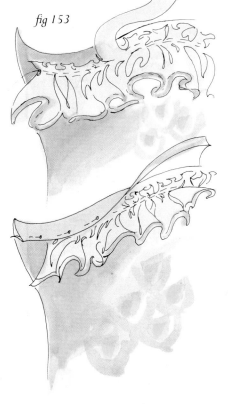

fig 152 Tacking the frill to the fold lines

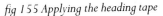

fig 153

fig 154 Trimming the raw edge of the frill and turning over the hem to form a bound edge

in a 6mm (¼in) double hem at the two side edges and along the bottom edge and machine stitch. Make two rows of gathering stitches 13mm (½in) from the top edge, dividing the strip into sections to distribute the gathers evenly.

4 Decide on the finished measurement of the curtain (include the frilled edge at the lower hem). Size up the curtain as for lined curtains (page 21) and fold down and press a 25mm (1in) hem allowance along the top edge where the heading tape will be positioned.

5 Open out the hem allowances at both sides and lower edges of the curtain fabric. With right sides together pin and tack the frill to the fold line on the curtain fabric, tacking along the gathering stitch line. Clip the curves around the corners. Distribute the gathers evenly but allow a little extra fullness at each corner so that the frill hangs well.

6 Trim the raw edge of the frill to 6mm (¼in) (fig 153) and turn over the hem allowance of the curtains to make a bound edge (fig 154). Slipstitch in position and press the seam towards the curtain fabric. Alternatively, tack the bound edge in position, press and topstitch on the right side of the curtain.

7 Turn over the top edge of the curtain to the wrong side, on the fold line, and apply the heading tape to the curtain (fig 155) following the instructions on pages 14-15.

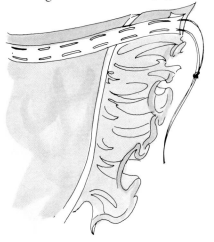

fig 155 Applying the heading tape

To make a double frill

1 For a 10cm (4in) double frill, cut strips of fabric on the straight grain, the required length for the frill, joining them with French seams if necessary. Turn in 6mm (¼in) double hems on the long sides, or for extra effect bind them with bias binding in a contrasting colour.

2 Fold the fabric in half lengthwise and work two rows of gathering stitches 3mm (⅛in) either side of the fold line (fig 156). (Divide the strip into sections of not more than 91.5cm (36in) so that it is easier to handle.)

3 Make up the curtain as for an unlined curtain (stage 1 above). Pin and tack the centre of the ruffle to the right side of the

fig 156 Forming a double frill

fig 157 Tacking the double frill in place

curtain, positioning it over the machined hems (fig 157). Machine stitch in position and remove the gathering stitches.

4 Turn over the top edge of the curtain to the wrong side, on the fold line, and apply the heading tape to the curtain following the instructions on pages 21-2.

SHOWER CURTAINS

These can be made in the same way as unlined curtains using PVC coated cotton or plastic waterproof material, or for the more luxurious effect shown here, polyester/cotton with a waterproof lining. When stitching plastic fabric hold the seams in place with sticky tape or paper clips, as pinning into it would damage the material. Machine rather than hand stitch, using a long stitch and a needle suitable for medium/heavyweight fabrics. Put a little tissue paper underneath the fabric to prevent it from sticking to the presser foot when working the seams.

Use synthetic heading tapes when making these curtains. Alternatively, make holes in plastic fabric with a special eyelet punch and thread through special plastic shower rings or hooks for fixing them to the rod or rail.

YOU WILL NEED

Fabric
Synthetic heading tape or eyelet punch and plastic rings

To make

1 Estimate the fabric needed for the curtains, allowing one and a half times the length of the rod. Measure the required depth of the curtain and allow 15cm (6in) for turnings at the top and lower edges (inclusive).

2 Turn in 13mm (½in) double hems at both side edges and a 25mm (1in) double hem at the lower edge of the curtains – and the top edge if using plastic material (fig 158).

3 Apply a synthetic curtain heading tape to the top edge of the curtains as for lined curtains (page 21) or punch holes in plastic material with a special eyelet punch (fig 158).

4 Alternatively, make detachable linings from nylon showerproof fabric and use them with cotton or lace curtains to match the decor of the room. Use a special detachable lining tape (fig 159) and hang the lining from the same rings as the curtains.

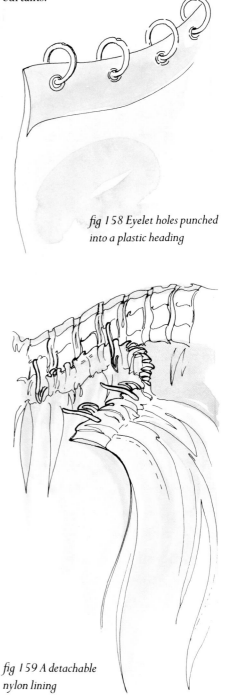

fig 158 Eyelet holes punched into a plastic heading

fig 159 A detachable nylon lining

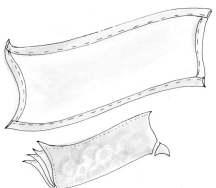

fig 160 *Making the cover for a hanger*

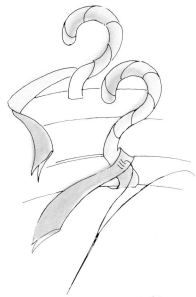

COVERED COAT HANGER

Not only can a padded hanger enhance your colour scheme with a matched or co-ordinated fabric, it helps your clothes keep their shape too.

YOU WILL NEED

Wooden coat hanger
Fabric to cover hanger
0·5m (½yd) fabric 90cm (36in) wide (to cover 4 hangers)
Matching thread
Strip of synthetic wadding
Clear adhesive
30·5cm (12in) Ribbon

To make

1 For a hanger 43cm (17in) long cut out a strip of cover fabric 50×15cm (19×6in) on the straight grain. Turn in a 6mm (¼in) double hem all round on to the wrong side and machine stitch in position (fig 160). Find the centre of the fabric by folding it in half lengthwise and then in quarters. Snip the corner to make a small hole (fig 160).

2 Cut a strip of the cover fabric 45·5cm × 13mm (18 × ½in) on the straight grain to bind the metal hook. Fold in one long side 3mm (⅛in) and press. Apply a little adhesive to the hook and bind it with the strip, overlapping it so that the raw edges are covered (fig 161). At the base of the hook wind the strip round the hanger and secure with a little adhesive and a few stitches (fig 161)

3 Cut a strip of wadding 10cm (4in) wide by the length of the hanger, plus 25mm (1in). Fold in half lengthwise. Stitch to the hanger (fig 162), turning in 13mm (½in) at both ends. Oversew in place.

4 Slip the cover fabric over the hanger through the hole in the centre. Pin the hemmed edges together and stitch with a double thread and a running stitch, gathering the fabric as in fig 163.

5 Attach a ribbon bow and trim (fig 164).

fig 161 *Binding the hook with fabric*

fig 162

fig 163

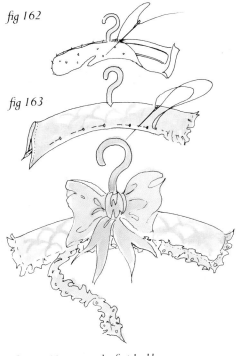

fig 164 *Trimming the finished hanger*

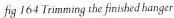

83

BOXED CUSHIONS

Boxed cushions have a trim, firm appearance. They are generally used for armchairs and other comfortable seating units, but their usefulness can extend to other areas. See, for example, pages 54-5 where two boxed cushions have been made up into oblong shapes, suspended on a strong curtain pole and used as a substitute for a wooden headboard – much more comfortable for reading in bed!

This type of cushion looks particularly attractive when the seams are trimmed with piping. Different colours can be picked out from patterned fabrics and accentuated in this way. The piping can echo the colours of the main cushion cover fabric, or match up with other patterned furnishings in the room, such as blinds, curtains or tablecloths. Alternatively use a plain fabric for the main part of the cushion cover and trim it with piping in a strong contrasting colour. Grey and red look very effective next to each other, for example. Piping gives the cushion covers a very tailored appearance which fits in well in smart, unfussy rooms – a masculine bedroom, perhaps.

Boxed cushions may be square or rectangular and can be made to the exact size you require, which makes them very useful for fitting into window seats or alcoves. They are made from two pieces of fabric joined together by a welt or border. You will ensure a better fit and a smoother appearance if you make the welt from four separate pieces of fabric.

Different fillings may be used for this type of cushion, depending on whether a rigid or soft finish is required. Guide lines are given in the Introduction (page 17) to help you select suitable materials. Remember that if you use a solid filling, such as plastic or latex foam, it is especially important to leave quite a large opening in the cushion cover so that the pad can be easily inserted. Cover the foam with calico or cotton cover before putting on the outer case to protect it from crumbling and wear.

ROUND BOXED CUSHION WITH ZIP OPENING

This kind of cushion is useful for stools or chair seats in kitchens, bedrooms and bathrooms. Choose firm, closely woven furnishing fabrics that do not shrink or stretch. For the filling use either a plastic foam shape or a loose filling such as feather and down or a synthetic fibre fill wadding (see pages 23-4, *Round frilled cushion*). Insert a zip fastener in the welt to close the opening on the cushion.

YOU WILL NEED

1m (¼yd) fabric 120cm (48in) wide
Piping cord No 3
(boiled for 5 minutes and dried before use to
ensure it will not shrink when cleaned)
Cushion pad
Paper for pattern
Zip fastener
Large plate or tray
Zipper foot attachment for machine

To make

1 Make a paper pattern to the size of the cushion using a large plate or a tray to draw the circle (fig 165).

2 Using the pattern, cut out two circles of the cover fabric for the top and bottom sections allowing 13mm (½in) turning allowances all round. Centre any fabric design if necessary and mark the positions

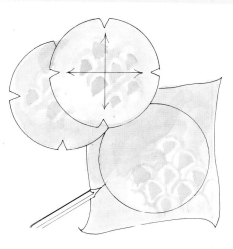

fig 165 Making the paper pattern. The fabric is notched on the straight grain

fig 166 The welt is cut in three sections to allow a zip fastener to be inserted

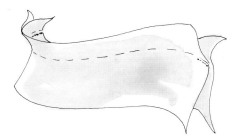

fig 167 Tacking sections 1 and 2 together and machine stitching the ends

for the ties on the bottom section. Notch both sections to mark the grain lines (fig 165).

3 Cut and prepare enough bias strips (38mm (1½in) wide) and piping cord to measure twice round the circumference of the cushion (use the quick method on page 109, Sewing Guide). Apply this to the top and bottom sections of the cushion as in figs 32 and 33 (*Floor cushion*, page 29), clipping the bias strip so that it moulds well round the curved edges.

4 Mark the position for the opening. This should be approximately a quarter of the circumference measurement of the cushion (usually about 23-25·5cm (9-10in) for this type of cushion).

5 Cut the welt in three sections on the straight grain of the fabric from selvedge to selvedge. For a welt measuring 75mm (3in) deep (finished measurement) cut two strips of fabric 50mm (2in) wide by the length of the opening plus 10cm (4in) (sections 1 and 2, fig 166). Cut a piece of fabric for section 3, 10cm (4in) deep by the length round the sides of the cushion from one end of the opening to the other (fig 166). Allow 13mm (½in) turnings at each end.

6 Insert a zip fastener between sections 1 and 2 as follows: tack a 13mm (½in) flat seam along two long sides of sections 1 and 2; machine the seam for 38mm (1½in) at each end (fig 167), but do not remove the tacking stitches (this is where the zip will be inserted); press the seam open.

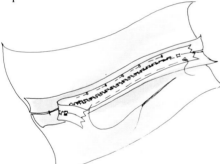

fig 168 Pinning and tacking the zip in place

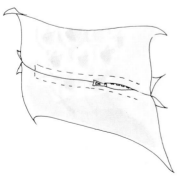

fig 169 The zip fastener is then machine stitched into place using a zipper foot attachment

7 Pin and tack the zip to the wrong side of the fabric, positioning it carefully over the tacked part of the seam (fig 168).

8 Turn the fabric to the right side and machine stitch the zip into position using the zipper foot attachment. Remove the tacking stitches from the seam to reveal the zip. Open the zip and finish the stitching (fig 169).

9 With the right sides together join one short side of the zipped welt section to one short side of welt section 3, ensuring the pattern is running in the same direction. Use a flat seam and take 13mm (½in) turnings. Notch the welt, and pin and tack it to the top section of the cushion cover, then find the exact position for the second join in the welt (fig 170). Pin, tack and machine the seams using a zipper foot attachment for the piped seam.

10 Open the zip and, with right sides facing, pin and tack the bottom section of the cushion to the lower edge of the welt matching the grain lines. Machine stitch into position and neaten the seams. Turn the cushion cover to the right side through the zip fastener opening and insert the cushion pad.

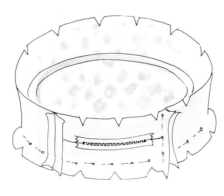

fig 170 The zip section is joined to the main section of the welt at one side only to allow for final adjustment for a perfect fit. The welt is notched and pinned and tacked to the top section of the cushion cover and the exact position for the second join in the welt section can then be established

You can give your towels a personal touch by decorating them to match curtains or blinds. Odds and ends of fabric left over from other soft furnishings you have made for your bathroom are ideal for this. Alternatively, pieces of lace or other trimming can be used, provided they wash well and are colourfast. A charming effect can be achieved by threading matching or contrasting ribbon through broderie anglaise as in the picture above. It is very important to choose fabrics which will not be scratchy or unpleasant to use next to your skin.

YOU WILL NEED

Towel
Fabric
or broderie anglaise and toning ribbon
Matching thread

To make
1 Cut four strips of fabric on the straight grain 64mm (2½in) wide by the width of the towel. Allow 13mm (½in) turnings at both ends.

2 Turn in and press 13mm (½in) at each side edge, then turn in 13mm (½in) at both long edges.

3 Tack and machine stitch to each end of the towel on each side.

A Feast of Fabrics

LINED BASKETS FOR BREAD
FABRIC COVERED WALLS
AUSTRIAN BLINDS
SQUAB CUSHIONS WITH TIES
TABLE NAPKINS

*Breakfast in style in the prettiest of rooms that really
makes the most of fabric in blinds, cloths, cushions and even wallcovering. A subtle summer garden design of blues and greens with the
merest touch of pink has been chosen for the walls, stretched on battens
and padded behind for a really luxurious effect, then used to make a
matching Austrian blind for the window, ruched and frilled against the
strong, blue painted woodwork.*

*A co-ordinating fabric in the same range of colours
but featuring an outsize flower print makes an attractive tablecloth
covered in a shorter, lace-edged cloth. A range of napkins in the same
basic shades of green and blue, but in a single striped material looks good
against plain white.*

*Judicious use of white maintains a light, fresh atmosphere:
white painted wickerwork chairs and plantstand suggest an almost
summerhouse effect; pure white china, blue, white and pink jugs and
vases for plants and flowers pick out the fabric shades. The cane chairs
have been made more comfortable for lingering meals by adding tie-on
squab cushions covered in fabric to match the walls. The final effect
blending the texture and colour range of co-ordinating designs is almost
one of a conservatory and creates the perfect place to eat a pleasant meal
at any time of the day or night.*

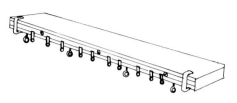

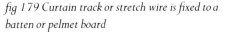

fig 179 Curtain track or stretch wire is fixed to a batten or pelmet board

fig 180 The frill is stitched at the lower edge then the blind is folded concertina-style to obtain straight lines for the tapes

AUSTRIAN BLINDS

These are sometimes called festoon blinds, as they are drawn up the window in swags. They are made in much the same way as Roman blinds (p. 97) but use more fabric as they are gathered both across the width and down the length of the blind.

The blind is hung from a curtain track or stretchwire which should be attached to the front of a wooden batten measuring approximately 50×25mm (2×1in) (fig 179). Fix this using angle irons underneath. The blind is pulled up the window by the cords which are threaded through the screw eyes and wound round a cleat (double) hook at one side of the window.

Before estimating the amount of fabric needed, decide whether to place the blind outside or inside the window recess. Use sheer or semi-sheer fabrics or any lightweight fabrics that drape well. Lining is optional. If using a patterned fabric, make sure that the pattern will lend itself to the scalloped style. Small random match patterns do not present any problems.

There is now a special kit available for making Austrian blinds, containing everything necessary for their construction.

To make a lightweight blind hang well, insert weights in the lower hem of the blind at the bottom of each length of vertical tape.

YOU WILL NEED

Fabric for blind
Matching thread
Austrian blind tape
Austrian blind cord, or strong nylon cord
Curtain heading tape with hooks
Cleat (double) hook
Screw eyes
Wooden batten 50×25mm (2×1in)

To make

1 Cut out the fabric, allowing twice the width of the window. For the length allow the depth of the window plus 45.5cm (18in). Join widths of fabric if necessary, matching patterns carefully and using French seams for unlined blinds. Position seams where they will be covered with a length of vertical tape and are as inconspicuous as possible (see stage 4 below).

2 Turn in 13mm (½in) double hems at sides and bottom edges.

3 To make the frill for the lower edge, cut out a strip of fabric 10cm (4in) by one and a half times to twice the fabric width. Make a 6mm (¼in) double hem along the two short sides and along one long side. On the other long side make two rows of gathering stitches and draw up to fit the bottom edge of the blind. Tack and machine stitch into position (fig 180).

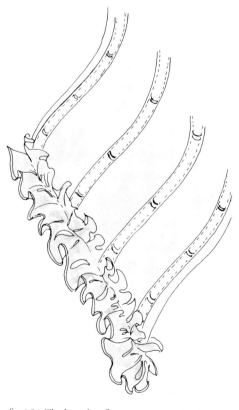

fig 181 The lengths of tape are sewn into place

4 Plan and mark the positions for the rows of vertical tapes. Either mark with a tacking line or, if the fabric allows, fold it concertina style and press it to obtain straight lines on which to tack the tape (fig 180). Position these from 25·5-61cm (10-24in) apart (remember that they will be approximately half this width when the blind is gathered up) and make the distances equal. If possible, cover any joins in the fabric by a length of tape.

5 Pin and tack the lengths of tape to the vertical guide lines. Start at the lower edge and make sure that a horizontal loop is positioned at the bottom of the blind on each length of tape, and that the loops are positioned evenly across the blind. Fold in each end of the tape 6mm (¼in) and machine stitch into position (fig 181).

6 Fold in 13mm (½in) at the top edge and apply a translucent pencil-pleated heading tape, or other curtain heading tape of your choice (fig 182).

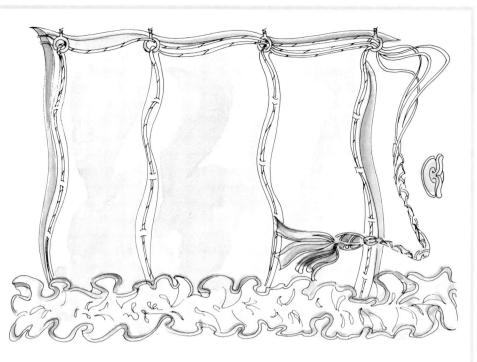

7 Pull up the cords on the heading tape to fit the width of the window and insert standard curtain hooks into the tape at approximately 75mm (3in) intervals. Fix the batten to the top of the window and position the screw eyes so that they are at the top of each length of vertical tape. Secure the cleat hook into position on the wall next to the blind.

8 Thread the cords through the loops on each length of vertical tape at the back of the blind as in fig 183, starting at the side of the blind opposite to where the cleat is positioned. Thread each cord through the screw eyes on the batten and knot the cords together, leaving enough loose cord for the blind to work easily. Do not cut off the excess cord but plait it together, knotting the end. This can be released easily when the blind needs cleaning. Hang the blind on the curtain track (fig 184). Draw it up the window and wind the cords round the cleat to secure it.

fig 183 The cords are threaded through the loops on each length of vertical tape at the back of the blind, starting at the bottom. Each cord is threaded through the screw eyes on the batten and then plaited loosely together to form one neat pull cord for operating the blind

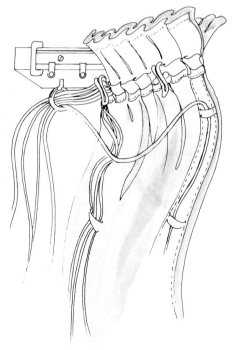

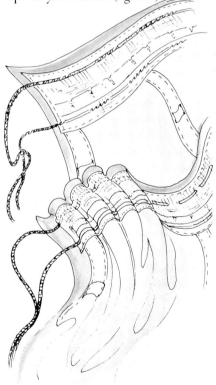

fig 182 At the top of the blind a translucent pencil-pleated heading tape is stitched into place. The cords are drawn up to fit the width of the window and curtain hooks are inserted at approximately 75mm (3in) intervals

SQUAB CUSHIONS WITH TIES

For full instructions see page 70.

TABLE NAPKINS

For full instructions see page 99.

fig 184 The screw eyes are positioned in the board so that they fall at the top of each vertical tape. The hooks are then inserted into the curtain track and the blind can be drawn up to the desired length

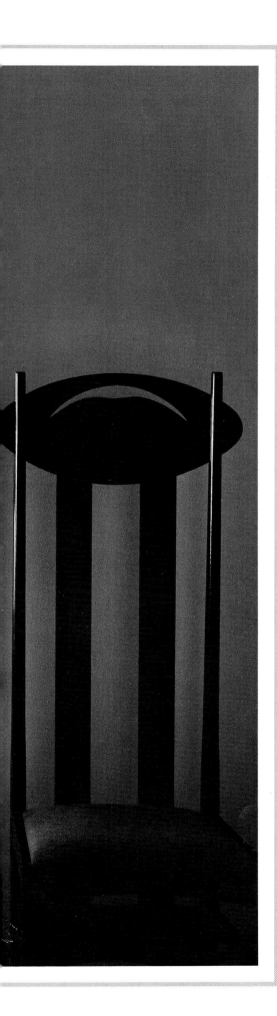

Timeless Elegance

ROMAN BLINDS
DINING CHAIR WITH DROP-IN SEAT
TABLE NAPKINS

If you have a particularly fine feature or striking piece of furniture, it really does pay to use it as the starting point when planning a scheme for a room. These magnificent high-backed dining chairs simply needed new drop-in seats and a coat of glossy black paint to make them the focal point of this simple but dramatic dining room.

With a monochromatic scheme of black and white, food takes on a vibrant quality, glowing with life and colour, and concentrates the attention wonderfully on the culinary delights to come. Meanwhile, the striking shape of the chairs is highlighted against a very subtly stippled grey wall, an all-white window providing a solid block of light in contrast with white woodwork and a plain white Roman blind for simple but practical decoration.

Keeping the shades of a black and white theme, the stylish table is highly polished black ash topped with elegant white crockery with a simple silver band, plain grey tray and an unusual black mesh fruit bowl.

This is a room that will never age, maintaining a quiet dignity and a chameleon-like quality that allows the emphasis of the scheme to change at will simply by adding a change of colour for flowers or napkins to bright red, golden yellow or even pink to suit the occasion and your mood.

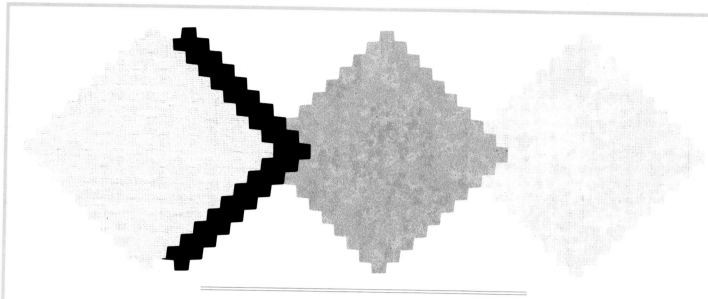

SAMPLES OF THE MATERIALS USED

1 Roman blind
Pure white 100% cotton with an embossed diamond pattern.

2 Chairs
Black gloss paint on woodwork provides a smart and striking contrast.

3 Wallcoverings
Washable grey wallpaper adds an interesting marbled finish.

4 Napkins
Washable white 100% cotton softly echoing the wallcovering.

AN ALTERNATIVE COLOUR SCHEME

Introduce a single splash of colour to a strict, monochromatic colour scheme and you create something both startling and dramatic. Here a judicious touch of shocking pink adds warmth and vitality to an otherwise sombre collection of grey tones, and changes the mood of the room completely. Creamy cotton fabric with wild random streaks of bright pink will make the blind a stunning focal point, matched to a similarly streaked charcoal grey and pink material made up into table napkins. For the rest of the room, keep to shades of grey to give the fabric most impact: a washable wallpaper in soft specked dove grey will provide a suitably neutral background for the more dramatic shapes and the colours of the fabrics; the striking chairs which can also be painted – a moody dark grey that is almost black. It is the shock of contrasts that works so well here: the well-ordered, restful quality of the soft greys broken by a single colour – the vivid pink, and by unexpected shapes and textures: the rough weave of the fabrics and the random nature of the design compared to the glossy finish and classic shape of the chairs. The secret is to strike that balance between your point of impact and the understated elegance of the rest of the scheme.

ROMAN BLINDS

Roman blinds fold up the window in pleats, and are similar in construction to Austrian blinds. They give a softer effect than roller blinds because they are drawn up the window in soft folds. They should be made from firm, closely woven curtain fabric and are best lined with curtain lining sateen. It is not necessary to stiffen the fabric for this type of blind. These blinds are fixed to a wooden batten approximately 50×25mm (2×1in) at the top of the window and when drawn up they are secured by winding round a cleat (double) hook at one side of the window.

Decide whether the blind is to hang inside or outside the window recess. If outside, add 64-75mm (2½-3in) extra to the finished measurement to make sure that it is wide enough to cover the window. If the blind is to hang inside the window recess make it approximately 25mm (1in) narrower than the width of the window so that it will fit the recess without difficulty.

Estimate the fabric needed by measuring the window or recess and allow 18cm (7in) (inclusive) for turnings at top and bottom hems, and 50mm (2in) (inclusive) for side hems.

YOU WILL NEED

Fabric for blind
Matching thread
Curtain lining sateen
Austrian blind cord, or strong nylon cord
Cleat (double) hook
Screw eyes
Narrow wooden lath or rod
Trimming (optional)
Tacks or staples for fixing the blind in position
Wooden batten 50×25mm (2×1in) for top of window (cover this with matching fabric if it is likely to show when the blind is in position)

To make

1 Cut out the blind fabric and the lining sateen to the size required, plus turning allowances, and place the two together

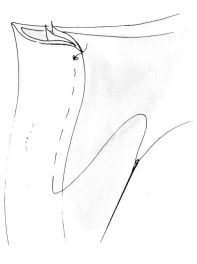

fig 185 *Turning in and tacking the fabric and the lining together*

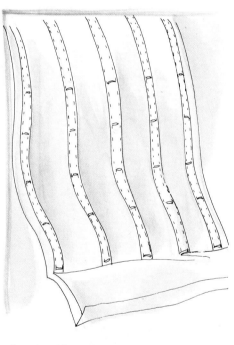

fig 186 *Folding the lower edge to make the casing. The vertical tapes are sewn in place*

with wrong sides facing. Fold in and tack both fabric and lining first 6mm (¼in) and then 13mm (½in) to make a hem at the side edges (fig 185).

2 Fold up 6mm (¼in) and then 10cm (4in) at the lower hem and press, but do not stitch in position (fig 186).

3 Mark the position for the rows of vertical tape, making the side guide lines 13mm (½in) from the side edges. Have the rows

equidistant and approximately 30·5cm (12in) apart. If the fabric allows, fold the blind concertina style and press it to obtain straight lines on which to sew the tape.

4 Tack the Austrian blind tape to the guide lines as in fig 186, positioning the ends at the lower edge of the hem. Make sure that a horizontal loop is positioned at the bottom of the blind on each length of tape (fig 181, *Austrian blinds*). Machine stitch into position through both layers of fabric.

5 At the lower edge tack and machine stitch the hem into position. Then make a casing for the wooden rod or lath by making a second row of machine stitching 32mm (1¼in) down from the first (fig 187). Insert the rod into the casing and slipstitch both side edges together to enclose it.

6 A trimming can be used to decorate the blind and this should be stitched on by hand to the two side and lower edges. Do not pull the stitches too tightly otherwise the trimming will pucker.

7 Fold over 13mm (½in) hem at the top edge of the blind and finish with a zigzag machine stitch.

8 Fix the batten to the top of the window and position the screw eyes so that they are at the top of each length of vertical tape. Secure the cleat hook into position on the wall next to the blind.

9 Thread up the blind as for the Austrian blind (fig 183, *Austrian blinds*), using strong nylon cord. Take each length of cord through the screw eyes on the batten. Knot the cords together leaving enough loose cord for the blind to work easily. Plait together the rest of the cord and knot the end.

10 Position the blind on to the batten and fix with tacks or staples (fig 188). Draw the blind up the window and wind the cords round the cleat hook to secure it.

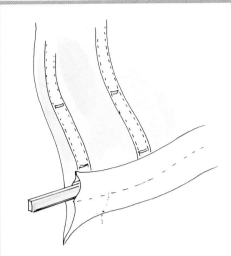

fig 187 *Inserting the wooden batten into the casing. The side edges should then be slipstitched to enclose the batten*

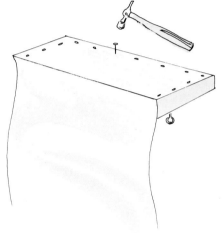

fig 188 *Fixing the blind to the board with tacks. A heavy staple gun could also be used*

DINING CHAIR WITH DROP-IN SEAT

This type of wooden dining chair has a separate seat which comprises a simple wooden frame with strips of webbing supporting the padding. The seat can be easily lifted out of the chair frame for repairs by taking out any dowels or screws that hold it in place and giving it a light tap with a hammer or mallet from underneath. The outer cover can then be replaced quite easily by stretching the new material over the frame and tacking it to the underside.

YOU WILL NEED

Upholstery fabric
Black upholstery linen or hessian
Chalk
Hammer
10mm (⅜) fine tacks

To make

1 Cut a piece of fabric large enough to go over the seat to the underside of the frame allowing 50mm (2in) extra all round. Make sure any pattern is centred.

2 Mark the middle at both front and back with a tiny nick. Place the fabric in a centred position on the top of the seat and turn it over to the underside (fig 189).

3 Mark the centre of the seat frame with chalk and pull the covering fabric over the rails at the front and back, aligning the nicks to the chalk marks (fig 189).

4 Insert a 10mm (⅜in) fine tack lightly at each point, and one at the centre of each side rail. Pulling the fabric tight, bang in a line of tacks at 50mm (2in) intervals.

5 Pull the fabric tightly towards the centre of the seat and insert a 10mm (⅜in) tack about 13mm (½in) from the corner. Cut into the excess fabric each side of the tack to form a tongue shape (fig 190a).

6 Pull one side of the fabric down over the tongue and anchor with two tacks about 25mm (1in) apart (fig 190b). Trim to 13mm (½in) from the tacks (fig 190c).

7 Repeat for remaining side, 13mm (½in) from the line of the tacks and about 50mm (2in) from the corner (fig 190d).

8 Cut a piece of black upholstery linen or hessian to fit the underside of the seat and adding 38mm (1½in) all round.

9 Turn under a 6mm (¼in) hem and fasten down over the existing tacks using 13mm (½in) fine tacks at 25mm (1in) intervals, making single square corners with turned edges (fig 191).

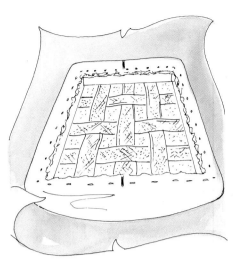

fig 189 *Aligning the centre of the seat frame with the straight grain of the fabric*

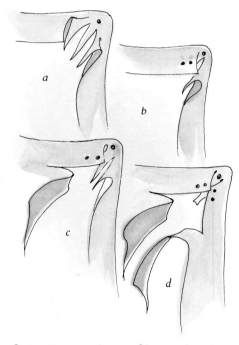

fig 190 *Fastening the cover fabric neatly at the corners*

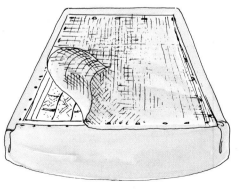

fig 191 *Tacking the black upholstery linen or hessian into position on the underside of the seat*

TABLE NAPKINS

Table napkins are easily made from square pieces of fabric, perhaps left over from other larger projects such as curtains, tablecloths or loose covers. Use easy-care washable fabrics in matching or co-ordinating colours and designs. Choose from polyester/cotton sheeting, furnishing cottons, dress fabrics and ginghams as well as man-made fabrics that wash well and are easy to iron. For a pretty, co-ordinated table-setting, why not make your table napkins in the same fabric as your table mats? (See page 76 for instructions on how to make *Oblong quilted place mats.*)

Finish raw edges with double-machined hems or bind them with bias binding. Alternatively, trim them with lace or other decorative edges, but make sure that these are washable. Even-weave fabrics can be machine stitched round all four sides 25mm (1in) from the raw edges and then frayed up to the stitching (fig 192).

Table napkins vary in size from 30·5-61cm (12-24in) square, but when using 90cm (36in) wide fabric a convenient size to cut is 45cm (18in) square. If using 120cm (48in) wide fabric the strip left at the side could be used for making bias strips to bind either mats, napkins or tablecloths.

YOU WILL NEED

1m (1yd) fabric 90cm (36in) wide (for 4 napkins approx. 40·5cm (16in) square)
Matching thread

To make

1 Cut four squares of fabric on the straight grain 45·5×45·5cm (18×18in).

2 Fold a 13mm (½in) double hem all round the napkin and press.

3 Tack and machine both sides of the hem. If using a zigzag stitch, first stitch along one side then turn the napkin over and stitch over the row again. Press well.

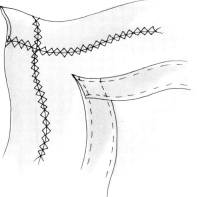

fig 193 *Sewing a double hem with a zigzag or straight machine stitch. First zigzag along one side, then turn over and zigzag over the original row of stitching. For a straight machine hem sew along the outside edge as well as along the hem line*

4 If using a small straight stitch, machine stitch once along the hem line, then make a second row of stitches close to the outside edge. Press well.

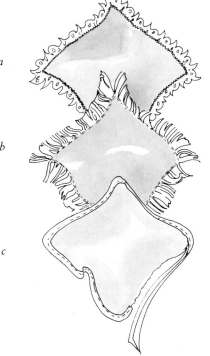

fig 192 *Three methods of neatening the raw edges on napkins (a) trimming with lace, (b) fringing, (c) applying a bias binding*

In the Classic Style

CURTAINS WITH HAND-MADE
TRIPLE-PLEATED HEADING

CURTAIN TIE-BACKS

CLASSIC LAMPSHADE WITH
BALLOON LINING

DINING CHAIR WITH DROP-IN SEAT

There is nothing to better dining in style against a sumptuous classic background. This traditional dining room is warm and inviting, combining the dignity of fine furniture with elegant soft furnishings to make the perfect setting for your best crystal and china.

Walls are papered in a rich marbled red which gives a warm, pleasant glow after dark when lit by a single table-lamp and flickering candlelight. An oriental print is sufficient to break up the colour on one wall, picking out the warm red in a branch of blossom. French windows call for full floor-to-ceiling curtains to make the most of their dimensions and these are beautifully framed by generous sweeps of fabric in a smart terracotta and blue striped design, the heading triple pleated by hand for a particularly opulent effect, and held away from the window on either side by matching tie-backs.

Good, traditional furniture is timeless and will only improve with age, but while wood matures, the fabric seats often begin to wear and look rather tired. Turn this to advantage by re-covering drop-in seats with fabric to match your scheme, or re-cover a collection of non-matching chairs in the same wood to make a set. Here a traditional style mahogany sideboard and table are dressed for dinner with chairs re-covered in the same striped fabric as the curtains for a smartly classical co-ordinated look.

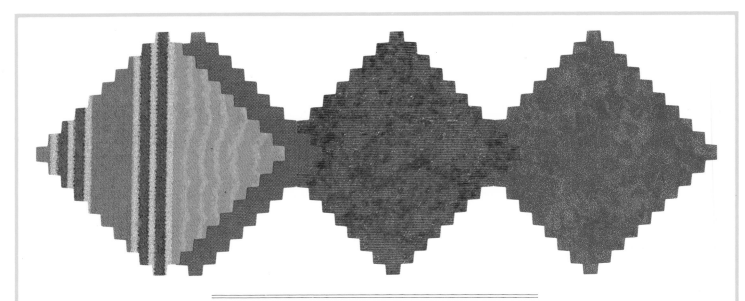

SAMPLES OF THE MATERIALS USED

---

1 Curtains, tie-backs, and drop-in seat covers
Blue, terracotta, brown and gold Regency stripe in 100% washable
cotton with the appearance of watered silk.

2 Lampshade trimming
Dark brown velvet picks up the thin stripe of the curtains.

3 Lampshade
Terracotta raw silk in the warmer shade of the main fabric.

4 Wallcovering
Glowing red washable paper with marbled finish provides the rich
background this scheme requires.

AN ALTERNATIVE COLOUR SCHEME

You can capture that same elegant atmosphere in the dining room with a similar mixture of plain and patterned materials, but using a cleverly co-ordinated scheme of navy, burgundy and cream. For rooms of less generous proportions substitute this smaller sprigged stripe design in burgundy and cream to echo the warmth of the mahogany furniture and still maintain that traditional feel. The fabric is fully washable cotton in a smart yet unfussy design which is ideal for making those generously swagged curtains with matching tie-backs and for re-covering the drop-in seats on the dining chairs. To provide an almost neutral background for a beautifully laid dinner table and finely dressed window, the walls should be cream too, maybe covered in this subtle marble effect wallpaper – the perfect foil for the deeper shades. It looks particularly fine in the warm glow of a plain lampshade in burgundy fabric, the colour picked out from the design on the patterned material. As the final touch, add piping and trimmings in plain navy blue fabric which makes a strong but dignified contrast to the burgundy and cream. Traditional furniture needs strong, plain colours and non-flowery designs to set them off to their best, classical advantage.

CURTAINS WITH HAND-MADE TRIPLE-PLEATED HEADING

Hand-made pleating looks very professional when used on curtains, blinds and pelmets. The heading of the curtain is stiffened with a special curtain-heading buckram or a non-woven interfacing. The pleats are then formed and stitched permanently in place. The heading of the curtains must fit the track or pole precisely (not forgetting to include the overlap at the centre), and the pleats must be positioned evenly along the top of the curtains with one at each end.

YOU WILL NEED

Curtain fabric
Matching thread
Buckram or non-woven interfacing
1 stab-in pin hook for each set of pleats
Curtain lining sateen
Tailor's chalk

To make

1 Make the curtains as for lined or interlined curtains (pages 21 and 30). Allow twice to two and a half times the length of the track for the curtain width.

2 Stiffen the top of the curtain by cutting a strip of buckram to the length of the top of the curtain Pin and tack this in position, turning over the top edge of the curtain 38mm (1½in) (fig 194). Turn in the lining 25mm (1in), mitre the corners and slipstitch across the top edge (fig 195).

3 Plan out the pleating and the spaces on paper first and then mark out the top edge of the curtain with pins and tailor's chalk as in fig 196. Allow 15cm (6in) for each pleat, 38mm (1½in) at each end and a 9-12·5cm (3½-5in) space between each one. Allow approximately five pleats per width of curtain. If necessary, adjust the size of the spaces between the pleats to fit into the available measurement by folding the curtain in half to mark the centre pleat first. Divide each pleat into three and mark with tailor's tacks.

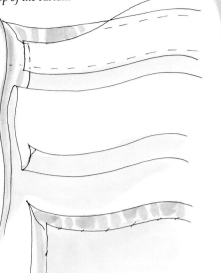

fig 194 Pinnng and tacking the buckram to the top of the curtain

fig 195 Mitring the corners and slipstitching the top edge

fig 196 Planning out the pleats

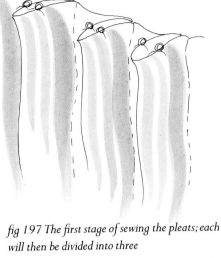

fig 197 The first stage of sewing the pleats; each will then be divided into three

fig 198 Securing the triple pleats

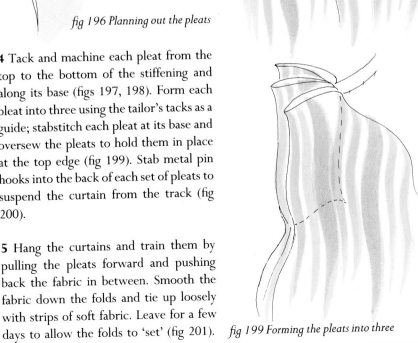

fig 199 Forming the pleats into three

4 Tack and machine each pleat from the top to the bottom of the stiffening and along its base (figs 197, 198). Form each pleat into three using the tailor's tacks as a guide; stabstitch each pleat at its base and oversew the pleats to hold them in place at the top edge (fig 199). Stab metal pin hooks into the back of each set of pleats to suspend the curtain from the track (fig 200).

5 Hang the curtains and train them by pulling the pleats forward and pushing back the fabric in between. Smooth the fabric down the folds and tie up loosely with strips of soft fabric. Leave for a few days to allow the folds to 'set' (fig 201).

2 From these measurements cut out a paper pattern and use this to cut out the pelmet buckram to its exact size (fig 203). Cut out the face fabric allowing 25mm (1in) turnings all round and cut out the interlining and the lining sateen allowing 13mm (½in) turnings all round.

fig 200 Stabbing pin hooks into the pleats

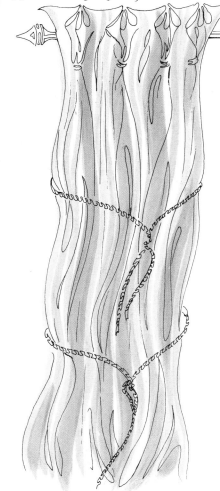

fig 201 Training the folds of the curtain

CURTAIN TIE-BACKS

Tie-backs are used to hold back curtains from the windows to let in the maximum amount of light, but they are also very decorative features and can be ruffled or shaped depending on the style of the curtains. Use fabric to match the curtains and trim with binding, braids or fringes; stiffen with pelmet buckram or non-woven interfacing. Alternatively use a PVC backing especially made for pelmets and tie-backs. Hang the curtains before measuring and making the tie-backs.

YOU WILL NEED

Pelmet buckram (or buckram, non-woven interfacing or PVC pelmet backing)
Cotton interlining (thick, fluffy bump or less bulky domette)
Face fabric
Matching thread
Curtain lining sateen
Metal or plastic curtain rings

To make

1 Decide on the length of the tie-back by tying a piece of string or fabric round the curtain, adjusting it to get the best effect (fig 202). Take care that it is not too short as this will crease the curtain. Decide on the width — from 5-10cm (2-4in) — and the shape of the tie-back by experimenting with different paper shapes before cutting out the fabric.

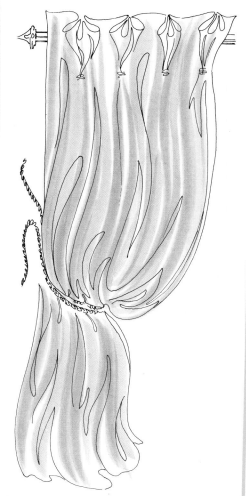

fig 202 Establishing the size of the tie-back

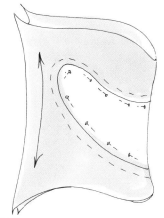

fig 203 Pinning the pattern on the straight grain of the fabric

3 Place the buckram on to the interlining and dampen the edges all round. Fold over the interlining and press with a hot iron so that it adheres to the buckram (fig 204). Slash curves or clip corners as necessary.

4 Lay the interlining face down on to the wrong side of the face fabric. Fold over the raw edges on to the buckram, dampen and press as before, slashing curves and mitring corners where necessary (fig 205).

5 Sew on rings at each end of the tie-back using strong thread and a buttonhole stitch. Fold in the lining fabric 13mm (½in) all round and apply to the back of the tie-back, slipstitching into position as in fig 206.

6 If using non-woven interfacing to stiffen the tie-back, secure it to the face fabric and interlining with herringbone stitch and finish as in stage 4 above.

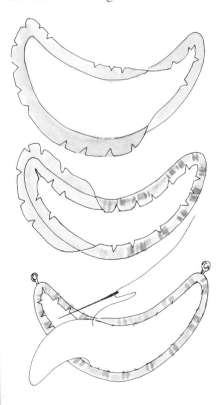

fig 204 *Pressing the interlining to the buckram*

fig 205 *Turning in the face fabric*

fig 206 *Slipstitching the lining in place*

CLASSIC LAMPSHADE WITH BALLOON LINING

This method can be used for most straight-sided and curved styles of frame where the measurement round the narrowest part of the frame is not greater than that round the top ring. The cover and lining are prepared using double fabric and are pinned on to one half of the frame only. The cover is stitched into position before the lining is inserted. For full details on choosing fabric and frame, see pages 16-17.

YOU WILL NEED

25·5-30·5cm (10-12in) bowed empire frame
Lampshade tape
0·5m (½yd) fabric 90cm (36in) wide for the outer cover
0·5m (½yd) fabric 90cm (36in) wide for the lining
Matching thread
Good quality steel dressmaking pins or glass-headed pins
Trimming

To make

1 Bind the frame with tape as in fig 24, page 25. Tape each strut first, making sure that the tape is tight and smooth. Start at the top ring and when the bottom ring is reached, wind the tape first to one side of the strut and then to the other, finishing with a knot around the bottom ring. Trim off the tape. When the struts have been bound, tape the top and bottom rings in the same way, making a figure-of-eight turn round each join in the struts and ring.

2 Fold the fabric in half and pin together with right sides facing. Place on to one half of the frame with the grain running down the middle of the frame as in fig 207. Pin the fabric to the side struts, placing the pins in the fabric every 25mm (1in) and having the heads in the position shown in fig 208. This makes it easier to tighten the fabric. Gently stretch the fabric and adjust the pins until the fullness is removed. Pin the fabric at the top and bottom rings, stretching it until all wrinkles are gone and the fabric is taut over the frame. Complete the pinning at the side struts so that the pins are 6mm (¼in) apart.

3 Draw a faint line with a pencil down the side struts, extending this line 13mm

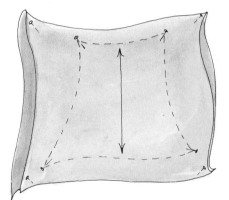

fig 207 *Pinning the folded fabric to the frame*

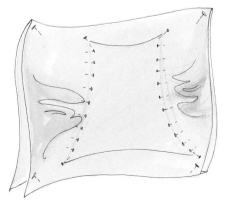

fig 208 *Easing the fabric to fit the frame and pinning at regular intervals*

(½in) at both top and bottom rings. This is the stitching line. Make a horizontal guide line either side of your pinned shape as in fig 209 and tack the fabric approximately 25mm (1in) from the pins on the side struts. Remove all the pins from the fabric and machine stitch down the pencil line (but not across the horizontal guide lines), using a medium-sized stitch. Trim both seams to 6mm (¼in) and cut across the fold line at the top. Press flat.

4 Prepare the fabric for the lining in the same way but stitch the seams 3mm (⅛in) inside the pencil lines.

5 Slip the cover fabric over the top of the frame and pin in position, matching the seams to the side struts and the horizontal guide lines to the top and bottom rings. Adjust the pins and tighten the fabric until the cover fits closely.

6 Working from right to left, stitch the cover to the frame using short lengths of double matching thread (fig 210). Trim off surplus fabric at the top and bottom rings, cutting as close as possible to the stitching.

7 Insert the lining into the upturned shade and pin in position, matching the seams and the horizontal guide lines to the top and bottom rings. Tighten the lining by adjusting the pins, keeping them on the outer edge of the rings (fig 211). Unstitch the side seam or, if necessary, slash the fabric and spread it out to make it fit round the fitting at the top ring (fig 212).

8 Oversew the lining to the frame with double matching thread, keeping the stitches on the outer edges of the top and bottom rings so that they will be hidden by the trimming. Cut off surplus fabric close to stitching.

9 Neaten the fitting by cutting a strip of lining fabric 10×3·8cm (4×1½in) on the straight grain. Turn in the edges to make a strip 13mm (½in) wide and slip underneath the fitting. Pin and stitch in position (fig 213) and trim off close to stitching.

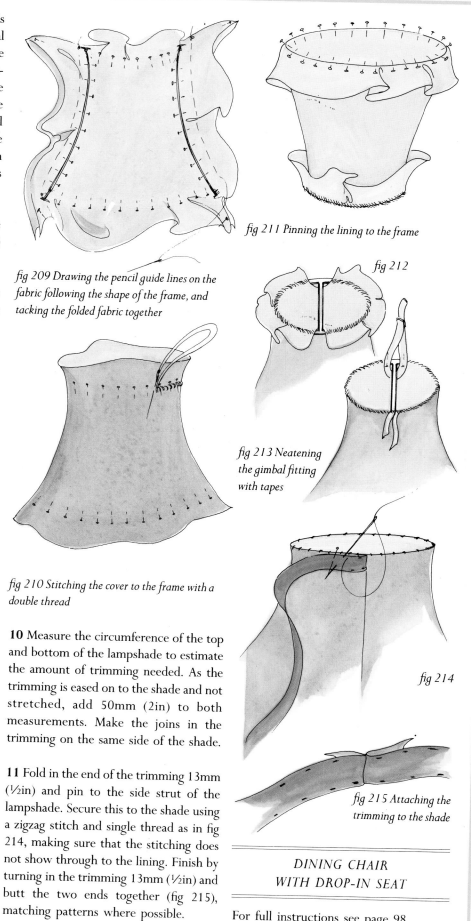

fig 209 Drawing the pencil guide lines on the fabric following the shape of the frame, and tacking the folded fabric together

fig 210 Stitching the cover to the frame with a double thread

fig 211 Pinning the lining to the frame

fig 212

fig 213 Neatening the gimbal fitting with tapes

fig 214

fig 215 Attaching the trimming to the shade

10 Measure the circumference of the top and bottom of the lampshade to estimate the amount of trimming needed. As the trimming is eased on to the shade and not stretched, add 50mm (2in) to both measurements. Make the joins in the trimming on the same side of the shade.

11 Fold in the end of the trimming 13mm (½in) and pin to the side strut of the lampshade. Secure this to the shade using a zigzag stitch and single thread as in fig 214, making sure that the stitching does not show through to the lining. Finish by turning in the trimming 13mm (½in) and butt the two ends together (fig 215), matching patterns where possible.

DINING CHAIR WITH DROP-IN SEAT

For full instructions see page 98.

Sewing Guide
With Hints on Care and Repair

STITCHES

Backstitch The needle is taken back the length of the stitch behind and brought through the length of the stitch in front working right to left. Use for strength and where it is not easy to use the machine. Keep the stitches even and about 6mm (¼in) long (fig 216).

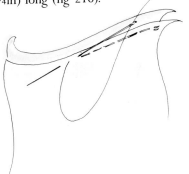

fig 216

Hemming The needle picks up a thread of fabric just under the fold and is inserted into the hem. Do not pull tightly. Work from right to left and on the wrong side of the fabric (fig 217).

fig 217

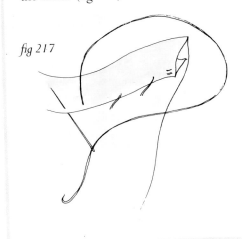

Herringbone stitch The stitch is worked from left to right in a criss-cross effect over the raw edge. Use to secure hems on interlined curtains. It is often used in appliqué as a decorative stitch, and also when making tie-backs with a non-woven interfacing (fig 218).

fig 218

Lockstitch A long, loose blanket stitch used to hold curtain linings and interlinings in position. Work from left to right, and position the stitches down the length of the curtain (fig 219).

fig 219

Outside tacking (slip tacking) Use this for matching patterns. An accurate match can be obtained by tacking the join on the right side of the fabric. Pin the two pieces of fabric together, matching the pattern. Tack on the right side of the fabric taking a stitch through the fold on the one side and into the single layer of fabric on the other (fig 220).

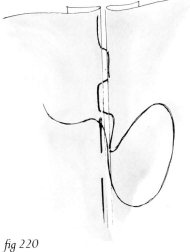

fig 220

Overcasting Thread taken over the edge of the fabric to prevent fraying. Neaten raw edges with overcasting if a machine with a swing needle (or zigzag stitch facility) is not available (fig 221).

fig 221

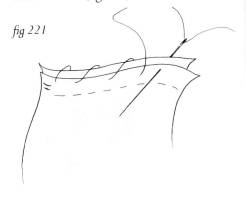

Running stitch Small, equal stitches worked from right to left. Can be used for gathering fabric by hand (fig 222).

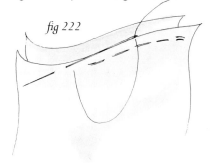

fig 222

Serge stitch Use when turning down a raw edge on a lined curtain. Work from left to right, picking up a thread from the curtain fabric and then a thread from the raw edge (fig 14 on page 21).

Slipstitch The needle picks up a thread in each fold of the two sides of fabric, sliding through the fold for 6mm (¼in) between the two stitches. Do not pull tight. Use for sewing folded edges together as in mitres, and also when stitching curtain linings in position (fig 195 on page 103).

Tacking Large, loose temporary stitches to hold two or more thicknesses of fabric together. Work from right to left, starting and finishing with a backstitch to secure (fig 223).

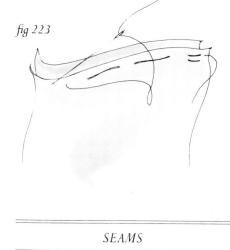

fig 223

SEAMS

Flat fell seam This is a strong seam which encloses raw edges. It is hardwearing, but the stitching shows on the right side of the fabric. Place the raw edges of the fabric together with the wrong sides facing.

Tack and machine 13mm (½in) from the edge and trim one side of the seam to 6mm (¼in) (fig 224). Turn in the other side of the seam 3mm (⅛in) and fold over the trimmed edge. Machine stitch along the fold on the right side of the fabric (fig 225).

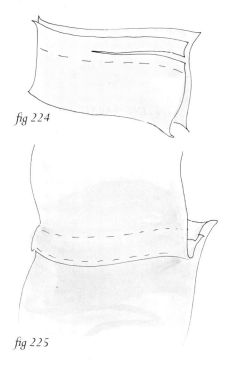

fig 224

fig 225

French seam Use a French seam where raw edges need to be enclosed, as on unlined curtains. However, this seam is only suitable for lightweight fabrics. Place the two raw edges together with wrong sides facing. Tack and machine stitch approximately 6-13mm (¼-½in) from the edges. Trim the seam and enclose the edges by placing the right sides of the fabric together. Tack and machine stitch (fig 226).

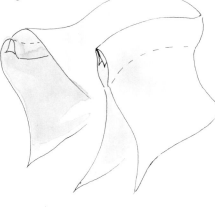

fig 226

Lapped seam Use this seam to join such fabrics as thick cotton, for instance, bump or domette, which have a tendency to stretch. Lap one raw edge of the fabric over the other and tack and machine using two rows of zigzag stitch (fig 227).

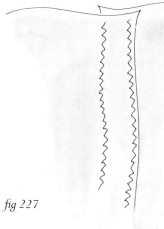

fig 227

Plain seam This is the seam most used in soft furnishings. Place the two raw edges of the fabric together, with the right sides facing. Tack and machine stitch 13mm (½in) from the edges. Neaten these where necessary with a zigzag machine stitch, or overcast them by hand (fig 228).

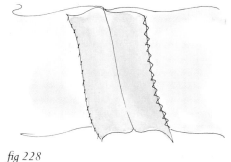

fig 228

MITRED CORNERS

A folded mitre is a neat way of finishing the corners on curtains, bedspreads and tablecloths. Make this using two hems of the same width.

Decorative trimmings are often applied to cushions, bedcovers, table napkins and so on. When they are applied parallel to the edge of the article it may be necessary to mitre them at the corners.

1 Fold in the hems and press them. Open out the fabric to show the fold marks (figs 229 and 230).

2 Fold over the corner of the fabric at right angles to the press marks (fig 231). If the fabric is thick, trim away some of the mitre to make it less bulky.

3 To complete the mitre, fold over the two hems on the pressing lines (fig 232). Secure the mitre by slipstitching the folds together (fig 233).

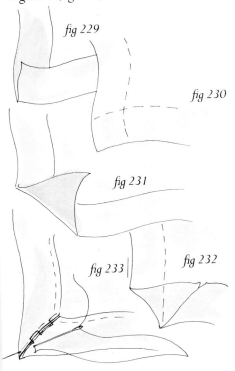

fig 229

fig 230

fig 231

fig 233   *fig 232*

PIPING CORD AND BIAS BINDING

Piping cord and bias binding are frequently used in soft furnishings; they both strengthen seams and make decorative edges for cushions and covers. Strips of fabric cut on the bias grain have more 'stretch' than those cut on the straight grain and are therefore more flexible and better able to be moulded round a curved edge.

Piping cord is available in various thicknesses from 1-6 (fine to coarse). To

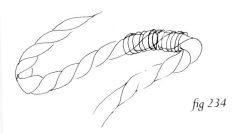

fig 234

make quite sure that cotton piping cord is fully shrunk, boil it for five minutes in a saucepan of water and dry thoroughly before use. Nos 2 and 3 piping cords are the ones most used in soft furnishings, and bias strip 38mm (1½in) wide is needed to cover them. Join the piping cord by cutting it and butting the two ends together. Wind a thread round them to secure them in position, making sure that they do not overlap (fig 234), as this would make a bulky seam.

CUTTING FABRIC ON THE BIAS GRAIN

1 Fold the fabric diagonally, so that it is on the true bias grain. Cut along the fold and use a ruler 38mm (1½in) wide to make strips suitable for covering piping cord (fig 235).

2 Make joins in bias strips on the straight grain of the fabric. Place two strips together with right sides facing, and pin them so that the seam produces an angle as shown in fig 236. Press the seam open and trim the corners as in fig 237.

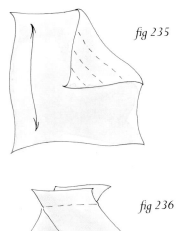

fig 235

fig 236

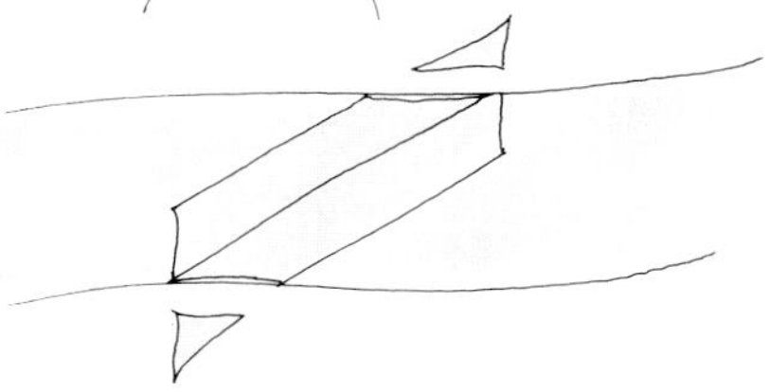

fig 237

QUICK METHOD OF MAKING BIAS BINDING

When long lengths of bias binding are needed for making covers, bedspreads or cushions, use the following method of joining the strips before cutting them. Once mastered, this method saves time and effort. A quarter of a metre (or ¼yd) of fabric makes approximately 5 metres (or 5yds) of bias strip 38mm (1½in) wide.

1 Use a strip of fabric 25.5cm (10in) wide by 56cm (22in) long. The length of the strip must be at least twice its width. Fold over the top right hand corner and the bottom left hand corner and cut along both folded edges (fig 238).

2 Using a ruler 38mm (1½in) wide, mark parallel lines on the fabric with a sharp piece of tailor's chalk, starting at the top edge. Mark a seam allowance of 6mm (¼in) down each side, and mark the first line at the right hand side 'A' and the second line at the left hand side 'B' (fig 238).

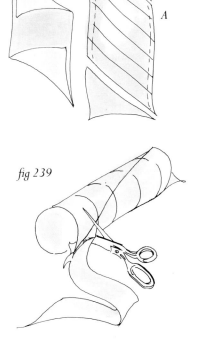

fig 238

B

A

fig 239

3 Insert a pin on the wrong side of the fabric exactly at point 'A' and take it across to 'B'. Insert the pin exactly at point 'B', having the right sides of the fabric together. Pin along the seam.

4 Turn the tube to the right side to check that the lines match up accurately. Tack and machine stitch the seam and press it open.

5 Turn the tube to the right side and start cutting at the top edge where the strip projects (fig 239).

6 The triangular sections of fabric cut from the original rectangular piece of fabric can be used in the same way. Join them as in fig 240, and proceed as in steps 1-3 above.

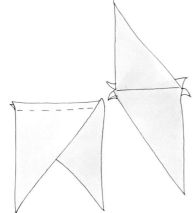

fig 240

CARE AND MAINTENANCE OF SOFT FURNISHINGS

When choosing soft furnishings, always look for fabrics that suit their particular purpose so that they are more able to withstand the inevitable wear and tear. Remember too that plain fabrics show the dirt more readily than patterned ones; smooth-surfaced and shiny fabrics repel dust better than textured or slub fabrics.

Since dirt and dust break down the fibres of all fabrics and make them wear out more quickly it pays to keep your home as dust-free and clean as possible to help preserve them longer. Regular care and attention will not only keep soft furnishings looking fresh but encourage them to give good service and look attractive for several years. With some items such as loose covers it is worth spraying the fabric with a fabric protector when new to help them stay clean.

Never pre-wash fabrics before making up curtains, festoon blinds, loose covers and other items as this can remove their fresh appearance and sometimes certain special finishes on the fabric making it soil more easily.

Make sure you know the fibre content of your fabric so that you can care for it in the appropriate way. If there is no 'care' label, check with the manufacturers. Instructions for washing and drying are also given on modern washing machines and washing powder packets.

Remove stains and spills from furnishing fabrics as soon as possible to prevent permanent marking. It is a good idea to find yourself a comprehensive stain removal guide and keep it handy for emergencies. As a general rule, colour-fast fabrics can be cleaned with a weak detergent solution or a proprietary cleaner, but always test first on a small piece of fabric that does not show. Or spray with a dry cleaning aerosol following the manufacturer's instructions.

IRONING

Keep the iron's surface perfectly clean by rubbing it with a non-abrasive scouring cream when the iron is turned off and is cold or use a proprietary cleaner.

Press fabric well at each stage of construction, removing tacking threads where possible as these can leave marks, and always use a piece of white cloth for pressing; this prevents scorching and shine on the fabric.

Check manufacturer's instructions for ironing each fabric but always test a sample piece before making up as temperatures vary from iron to iron. Start with the lowest temperature setting and increase it slowly until the correct setting is found.

Remember that velvet fabrics cannot normally be ironed but should be tumble dried. Take special care when pressing seams that the pile is not crushed; steam press from the reverse side and use a velvet board if possible.

LOOSE COVERS

When making loose covers, consider having the whole length of fabric pre-shrunk at a laundry before making up. The fabric is put through a steam roller which shrinks it without damaging its 'finish'. Never try to pre-shrink yourself by washing. If you allow a little extra fabric when estimating, you can use it for replacing worn sections and for making extra arm caps to help prolong the life of your covers.

If washable, iron loose covers while still damp – on the chair itself wherever possible. This reduces the chance of shrinkage. Press the frill first before putting the cover on to the chair.

CURTAINS

Most curtains are best dry-cleaned, except lightweight unlined ones that have good washing qualities.

Keep lined and interlined curtains regularly brushed, and vacuum them frequently, using the special attachments on the cleaner. Hanging them on the washing line on a fine day freshens them up too.

The pile on velvet curtains should lie upwards. They look better, mark less easily and do not hold dust.

Interlined curtains require specialist treatment, as they are constructed from three different fabrics. Each may require a different cleaning technique.

LAMPSHADES

Keep lampshades clean by brushing them regularly with a soft brush.

Bloodstains or fly marks can be removed from fabric shades by chewing a piece of tacking thread and rubbing it gently on the stain. This removes the stain without leaving a water mark.

Soft lampshades can be carefully washed, using a gentle detergent and warm water. Rinse well and hang on the washing line to dry on a good drying day.

Index

Acknowledgements

The author and publishers would like to thank the following companies for their contribution to this book:

for supplying merchandise for the room sets:

Collier Campbell Limited, Crown Wallpapers, Liberty & Co. Ltd, Osborne & Little Limited and Arthur Sanderson and Sons Ltd.

for supplying props for the room sets:

Le Cadeau, Dafna Designs, Gold & Fox Limited, Kiwi Fruits, The Poster Shop, The Towel Centre, all at Covent Garden; The Gingerbread House, Buckingham (for Merrythought and Brio goods), Marks and Spencer plc.

Details of materials used in the room sets:

All paints are by Arthur Sanderson and Sons Ltd.

Fresh, Young and Bright (page 20): upholstery fabric, Arthur Sanderson & Sons Ltd; curtains and square cushion, Habitat; round cushion and piping, John Lewis Partnership; lampshade, John Lewis Partnership. Alternative colour scheme: upholstery fabric, round cushion, lampshade and piping, Designers Guild; curtains and square cushion, Pallu & Lake Furnishings Limited.

Invitation to Relax (page 28): all fabrics by Collier Campbell Ltd. (Collier Campbell fabrics are available from Liberty, Heals and leading stockists. There are about 400 throughout the country. Enquiries to Christian Fischbacher, 40 Clipstone Street, London W1.) Alternative colour scheme: upholstery fabric, John Lewis Partnership; curtains and cushions, Coloroll; scatter cushions and piping, Designers Guild.

Traditional Comfort (page 34): upholstery fabric and curtains, Arthur Sanderson and Sons Ltd; cushions, round tablecloth and piping, Designers Guild; wallpaper, Crown. Alternative colour scheme: upholstery, curtains, cushions, tablecloth and piping, Designers Guild; wallpaper, Arthur Sanderson & Sons Limited.

Waking Up to Summer (page 41): bed cover, valance, curtains, cushions, tablecloths and wallpaper, Laura Ashley Limited. Alternative colour scheme: bed cover, valance, curtains, cushions and tablecloths, Laura Ashley Limited; wallpaper, Osborne & Little Limited.

The Tailored Touch (page 52): bed cover, headboard cover, curtains and pelmet, ottoman cover and piping, Designers Guild; wallpaper, Arthur Sanderson and Sons Ltd. Alternative colour scheme: Fabrics and wall covering from the Dolly Mixtures collection by Coloroll; piping, Designers Guild.

Colourfully to Bed (page 60): quilt cover, valance, headboard cover, curtains, pillow case and appliqué work, John Lewis Partnership. Alternative colour scheme: quilt cover, pillow case, curtains and piping, John Lewis Partnership; valance and headboard cover, Laura Ashley Limited.

Country Cottage Charm (page 68): curtains, cushions and place mats, Liberty; piping, John Lewis Partnership. Alternative colour scheme: curtains, cushions, place mats and piping, Laura Ashley Limited.

A Place in the Sun (page 74): blind fabric and kitchen accessories, John Lewis Partnership; binding, Designers Guild. Alternative colour scheme: blind, accessories and binding, Laura Ashley Limited; wallpaper, Crown.

Pretty and Cool (page 80): curtains, cushions and piping, Laura Ashley Limited. Alternative colour scheme: curtains, cushions and piping, Laura Ashley Limited; wallpaper, Designers Guild.

A Feast of Fabrics (page 88): wallcovering, Austrian blind, tablecloth and napkins, Designers Guild. Alternative colour scheme: wallcovering, Austrian blind, tablecloth and napkins, Laura Ashley Limited.

Timeless Elegance (page 96): blind fabric, Pallu & Lake Furnishings Limited; wallpaper and napkins, Osborne & Little Limited. Alternative colour scheme: blind fabric and napkins, Designers Guild; wallpaper, Crown.

In the Classic Style (page 102): curtains and seat covers, lampshade and wallpaper, Osborne & Little Limited; lampshade trimming, John Lewis Partnership. Alternative colour scheme: curtains and seat covers, Laura Ashley Limited; lampshade and lampshade trimming, Coloroll; wallpaper, Osborne & Little Limited.

The publishers also wish to thank the following organizations for their kind permission to reproduce photographs in this book: Designers Guild, pages 6, 10 and 16; Dorma, page 8: Pallu & Lake Furnishings Limited, page 15; Arthur Sanderson & Sons Limited, page 9.

Special photography and jacket by Paul Williams.

Illustrations by Caroline Holmes-Smith (Artist Partners).

Soft furnishing in room sets made up by Ferguson Decor.